Still Magic

A **gin distiller's guide** for beginners

MARCEL THOMPSON

R3THINK PRESS

First published in Great Britain in 2019
by Rethink Press (www.rethinkpress.com)

Image credits

Cover image © Dominik Maier / Adobe Stock
p15 © Adobe Stock
p199 © Lauren Orrell, www.laurenophotography.com.au
p82, p126 graphic design by Julia Gamble Vale,
juliagamblevale@gmail.com

Disclaimer

In many countries you will require a licence to distil alcohol. There are some exceptions; New Zealand is a case in point. Obtaining a licence to distil, and meeting local compliance criteria, is now a simple process, especially with the prevalence of online services.

It is important to check the legal status of amateur distillation in your country before embarking on your own distilling journey – and never produce alcohol for sale without a licence.

Contents

Foreword

Starting a distillery isn't easy. Prior to launching Four Pillars in late 2013, we spent nearly two years planning and piecing together the distillery. I always call this our *Breaking Bad* phase. Although we had production experience in the wine industry, we were largely flying blind.

Something we realised very early on was the lack of a strong and willing knowledge bank in Australia. There were not many distilleries and even fewer specialising in gin.

Sure, it's a mountain of fun: choosing botanicals, distilling, creating recipes, making drinks… but after a while you find yourself with more questions than answers. It's a classic case of picking a stitch and ending up doing surgery.

Almost every week someone visits our distillery with the ambition of making gin, but the divide between ambition and ability is often glaring. To this day, I often wonder how people approach this industry without any production experience or palate training.

Little did I know that Marcel Thompson was sitting on my doorstep. Here is a man who has distilled two of the world's most historical and important gin brands: Tanqueray and Gordon's! He has a mountain of experience in large and small operations, R&D, palate development and so much more. More recently, he's partnered with Jesse Kennedy and Griff Blumer to create the Poor Toms product range. And somewhere along the way he found time to write this book.

When you meet Marcel you instantly realise he's a real character with an unbridled passion for gin. He has story after story about projects he has worked on, and he isn't afraid to share his experience and knowledge. *Still Magic* just confirms his generosity.

Few people are better placed to offer the advice he shares in this book. He starts with some basic set-up advice before launching into a step-by-step guide to recipe creation and so much more. I kept thinking to myself, 'Geez, I wish I'd done that! I might have launched sooner.'

His constant reinforcement of key principles is crucial.

But this book isn't just for would-be distillers. This is a great book for anyone looking to start a business, anyone interested in creating something – the principles don't really change.

I look forward to recommending this book when would-be distillers come knocking. Well done mate, you're a legend.

Cameron Mackenzie
Founder and Distiller
Four Pillars Gin
www.fourpillarsgin.com.au

Introduction

Gin. One of the shortest words in the alcohol lexicon, yet one of the most enduring. It takes its name in equal measure by channelling words from the Dutch and French languages, and the botanical name of a fabulous plant.

If you love gin and want to know how to make it, this book will show you how. You will learn about relevant gin techniques that have stood the test of time, and the part they play in today's global resurgence. You'll receive a distiller's view of the gin world, paying homage to its colourful history, its place today, and what gin's future would look like with you at that helm. Gin is still magic today as it ever was.

Following graduation from Auckland University in the 1980s, I took up my first career role as an assistant distiller. Without fully appreciating this at the time, I was fortunate enough to be apprentice to some of the legends of Australasian gin making, whose gin making lineage can be traced back to the giants of the game in pre-war Britain. This experience provided me with a springboard into related roles over time, ranging from manufacturing, production and quality control oversight, to driving new product development ideas from concept to commercialisation.

I've held end-to-end product development and delivery responsibilities for many products during my career, but my enduring passion has lain with gin making for local and international consumption. This includes producing Gordon's, Tanqueray, Booths and Vickers as key experiences garnered at an early age.

My interest in the alcohol industry and a thirst for knowledge led to joint venture project roles with United Distillers (Aust) Ltd (now Diageo), International Bottling Company, New Zealand Wines & Spirits, Fairdeal Liquors, and the Punja Group of Companies; a clear case for describing the benefits of volunteering writ large.

The projects focused upon new products in new markets, and the creation of compliant systems for joint venture partners. Understanding and delivering upon customer expectations have been key success factors to date.

In more recent times, I've taken on the Gin Mastermind mantle at Poor Toms Gin, a craft distillery located in inner Sydney, Australia.

This role allows me to express and share my passion for three key concepts; making gin more accessible to its manifold enthusiasts, safeguarding gin's commercial success and creating an enduring mark for generations to come.

Heritage. Guardianship. Legacy.

To some extent writing this book is a by-product of subscribing to those three key concepts. However, it was the serendipitous meeting with three keen gin enthusiasts and a misadventure that catalysed my motivation to transform this belief into one of personal commitment; to bring Heritage, Guardianship and Legacy to life in a different time and space.

What I describe next has the potential to be one of 'those' jokes that people tell one another, that often end badly. Spoiler alert; this one does not.

In October 2014 a banker, an actor, and a business owner walk into a bar – in Chatswood, Sydney – to meet yours truly. I met two entrepreneurs colloquially referred to as the Poor Toms: Jesse Thomas Kennedy, and Griffin Thomas Blumer. Both young men took the courageous decision to walk away from their careers and pursue a dream; to make world class, playfully irreverent gin. Armed with little more than small stills and lofty ideas, their energy, enthusiasm and desire were the first characteristics that struck me. These are inherent and are nigh impossible to teach; however, they also make people very teachable when directed in a collaborative fashion. As far as I can tell it would be unlikely that anyone has tried – or ever will – to describe what I had in mind. A crash course in scalable gin making techniques became the order of the day; February 2015 signalled the start of weekend-based Gin Making Boot Camps.

Then came the misadventure; I felt a little unwell and sought medical advice. Symptoms were consistent with 'flu or some other viral ailment albeit inconclusive. Turns out it was a little more serious than first thought. It's often at times like these when people reflect inwardly, and this was no different. I had too much to do, not a lot of time to do it and was driven by the fear of letting the Poor Toms down before they'd started. Three important matters and a gin dream were at stake.

Poor Toms

A year-long chemotherapy campaign coupled with a modified gym program created by my personal trainer Troy McLellan lay ahead from Easter 2015. This left seven weekends to get the boot-camps up and running to meet the goal of producing world class gin.

I decided to fight and so did Poor Toms, resulting in award winning recognition at the 2016 San Francisco Spirits Competition for Sydney Dry Gin; the start of global and national accolades in subsequent years. In 2016, Fool Strength Gin was released and won gold medals in 2018 at the Australian Distilled Spirits Awards and The International Wines and Spirits Competition, London. In the latter case, Poor Toms was the second Australian product to achieve gold since the competition's inception in 1969.

My hope is that this book will help you start your gin making journey. You need little experience as energy, enthusiasm, desire and applying simple instructions will get you there. If you love gin, maybe something about cooking, and a little about music – or a lot for that matter – then this book is for you.

Gin has been the drink of aristocrats and everyday people since the seventeenth century. It is steeped in a rich history, driven by forces as diverse as the need for social connection, and warfare.

It is the product of both art and science with an unequalled heritage attracting a keen sense of guardianship among its enthusiasts.

Gin's resurgence in popularity in the twenty-first century serves to enrich a centuries-long standing tradition, thereby reinforcing its legacy for future generations to build upon.

There are recurring themes throughout every gin making journey; simplicity, common ground, record keeping, and legacy. Eating, drinking and making merriment are traditions that span centuries. You will see how intertwined these pursuits are and the commonality they share with gin making. In the age of sociability and connectedness that we now live in, it is both heartening and exciting to see where the next chapter in gin's centuries-long story will take us.

The four chapters of this book follow a gin making timeline.

Chapter One will show you how to make gin. It will transport you back in time to the heady days of early gin making and will help you understand and apply first principles. You will learn about botanicals, bases and blending: the 3Bs of gin making used by seventeenth century gin makers in London, gin's spiritual home.

Chapter Two will build upon the 3Bs and show you how to make distilled gin. You will learn about decision making, investigation, sampling, testing, improvements and launching; the D.I.S.T.I.L. process. This process represents the major technological step-change that drove gin production and consumption to unprecedented levels in eighteenth century London.

Chapter Three will provide examples of how access to modernised versions of nineteenth century technology gave rise to the massive production of globally significant gin brands that set the tone for twentieth century consumers. You will also see that toward the latter part of the twentieth century another technological step-change catalysed the small batch distilling movement to prominence in the twenty-first century. Chapter Three concludes by setting a challenge for you to consider.

Finally, Chapter Four discusses the essential considerations for a successful gin product launch and ends with a Glossary of gin making terms used by gin makers.

So, let's be Gin…

CHAPTER ONE

The Building Blocks Of Gin

Gin making requires an understanding of three building blocks which this book refers to as the 3Bs. This chapter will demonstrate how gin making is primarily a combination of art and science and will describe each of the 3Bs in turn:

1. Botanicals

2. Bases

3. Blending

You will also gather a high-level understanding of how these building blocks hold the key to past, present and future gin products.

Comparisons of gin making skills to the culinary arts and music are used to embellish your appreciation of the 3Bs and their application in the gin making process is demonstrated with five simple gin examples.

The 3Bs of gin making

As an initial first step, there are a few pieces of inexpensive equipment to have on hand. These will become important as you progress through the 3Bs:

- A set of kitchen scales, to weigh botanicals, say up to 100 grams.[1]

- A set of measuring spoons.

- An A5-size notebook to record information in a diary format.

- A measuring cone, like those used for measuring out liquid medication.

- A pipette for sampling purposes. A drinking straw, or a small polyethylene pipe connector are equally effective.

- A clean 500ml capacity water bottle. Repurposing a clean empty squeezable bottle is ideal.

---

1   This is key as the quantities to weigh will be fewer than 10 grams in most cases. A larger capacity weighing machine will make measuring small quantities very difficult.

Getting there is as much about enjoying the experience as arriving safely at your destination.

Make observation, relentless curiosity and tenacious note-taking your best friends.

The 3Bs of gin making – Botanicals

There is a vast array of botanicals available to all gin makers, each with specific nuances and flavours. Thankfully, gin makers have managed to group these botanicals into families or categories for ease of reference.

Botanicals, the essence of all gin making magic

After more than 300 years of relentless curiosity on the part of the gin making giants of history, we can be forever thankful that modern day distillers have taken up the reins in their stead. There are simple ways to describe the flavours that each botanical can provide in the finished gin.

- Floral
- Fruity
- Spicy
- Woody
- Herbal
- Nutty
- Citrus

From here the gin maker can make considered choices concerning the botanicals they intend to use. For example, the term 'floral' may mean using botanicals as varied as camomile, lavender, hibiscus or elderflower.

Botanical listings

Here is an alphabetical listing of botanicals that are in common use by gin makers all over the world. I've also included their scientific names and their generic plain English descriptions for additional reference. Botanicals form groups, and categories which is an invaluable insight to maintain.

From an operational ease viewpoint, the best supporting botanicals are the ones that are in ready supply, are easy to store if needed during off-seasons when supply is scarce, and relatively inexpensive.

In the same way that musical notes, key signatures and scales are the cornerstone of musical expression, these botanicals fill the same role for a budding gin maker.

Botanical listings

Common name	Botanical name	Easy description
Angelica root	Archangelica officinalis	Rooty
Aniseed	Pimpinella anisum	Nutty/Spiced
Bitter orange peel	Citrus aurantium	Citrusy
Calamus	Acorus calamus	Spiced
Caraway	Carum carvi	Grassy
Cardamom	Elettaria cardamomum	Spiced
Cassia	Cinnamomum cassia	Spiced
Cinnamon	Cinnamonum zeylanicum	Spiced

(Continued)

Common name	Botanical name	Easy description
Coriander seed	Coriandrum sativum	Spiced/Citrus
Cubeb berries	Piper cubeb	Spiced/Rooty
Fennel seed	Foeniculum vulgare	Grassy/Herbal
Grains of Paradise	Afromomum melegueta	Spiced/Rooty
Juniper berries	Juniperis communis	Herbal
Lemon peel	Citrus limon	Citrusy
Liquorice root	Glycyrrhiza glabra	Sweet
Nutmeg	Myristica fragrans	Nutty
Orris root	Iris pallida	Rooty
Sweet navel orange peel	Citrus sinensis	Citrusy

Chapter Two will provide a more comprehensive list of botanical groupings which helps to link a gin flavour outcome, with specific botanicals.

Botanicals provide the starting point and are key to bases for all gin making. This section will describe what botanicals are, and initial ways to group them for ease of reference. Examples taken from the culinary arts will demonstrate how different ingredients can describe an end-product, and how this principle applies to gin making.

Botanicals is the term used to describe the various ingredients that provide the flavour and aroma sources for all gin. They are naturally occurring materials, with flavour compounds, drawn predominantly from plant sources. There are some edgy operations in the craft distilling world that are using non-plant sources, thereby making the term botanical redundant in such cases.

Here's a closer look at the most important botanical of them all: juniper berries.

Juniper berries

These provide the cornerstone for all gin made everywhere by everyone.

Juniper berries are the fruit from a plant called the *Juniperus communis*. The flavours and aromas contained within the berries are what make gin 'gin'.

Juniper berries

The berries themselves are interesting, with each berry containing three seeds which are about 3–4mm in length. Use this reference point to find a more detailed view of juniper berries.[2]

Juniper berries provide the basis for the piney flavours and aromas associated with all gin. This should come as no surprise as by law, every gin must use juniper.

The juniper berry seeds are rich in fragrant aromas, comprising three main compounds, which in turn come from a family of compounds called terpenes.

Try taking a few juniper berries and cracking them open to reveal the seeds. It will become clear where gin's distinct flavour and aroma characteristics originate.

---

2   By Hardyplants at English Wikipedia – Own work, Public Domain, https://commons.wikimedia.org/w/index.php?curid=21033990

Their names describe their aroma to some extent:

- Limonene – a citrus aroma
- Alpha Pinene – a pine tree aroma
- Linalool – floral with some spiciness

Over the years, additional research into this berry has uncovered other fabulous compounds that describe its characteristics and, by extension, the nature of all gin aromas and flavours.[3]

Compounds

Compound	Flavour/Aroma Description
alpha pinene	piney
limonene	citrus
borneol, camphene, terpinene, cadinene	woodiness
cineole	mint
terpin-4-ol	nutmeg
caryophyllene	spiciness

Given that these compounds occur in nature and are available for advanced chemical analysis, my enthusiasm and curiosity was piqued. What if you could determine how much of each compound occurred in the berries? Could this mean it would be possible to make gin using the pure material compounds instead of botanicals? I thought I'd find out.

GAS CHROMATOGRAPHY, QUALITY AND SYNGYN

Following graduation as a chemist in 1987, the chance to take up a role as an assistant distiller with the New Zealand Distilling Company arose. At the time the business focused on adopting and reinforcing a scientific approach to quality control. Coupled with learning the tools of the trade the challenges were interesting, exciting and relevant.

Part of the role involved the use of a chemical analysis technique called gas chromatography, primarily to monitor the quality of incoming raw materials. There were two companies in New Zealand's North Island whose core business was to produce high quality alcohol for use by the spirits industry. The need to source raw materials, yeast, fermenters and other machinery fell to the company's joint venture partners at Edgecumbe and Reporoa, located in New Zealand's Bay of Plenty. They made high quality alcohol for use in distilling operations, meaning there was no need for the business to create its own alcohol base. The characteristics from each partner were subtly different, despite using similar raw materials and processing methods. These differences took some time to understand and appreciate via traditional organoleptic testing approaches. (Organoleptic testing is explored in more detail later in this chapter.) The thinking at the time was that if technology could help determine quality compliance quickly and accurately, then the business benefits would warrant the investment.

Gas chromatography is a powerful tool of the trade for any chemist and it provides a chemical analysis, crudely like a fingerprint. Part of the role included commissioning this new technology so that the results were accurate, precise, repeatable and timely.

The outcome of this work represented a step-change; qualitatively assessing neutral alcohol consignments now had both the experienced olfactory approach, and a technical approach to support the team's observations.

By extension I tried to apply the same principles to gin making, in efforts to find the 'fingerprints' for assorted gin products. My research then led to understanding all the various flavour components that gins possess and procuring standards from chemical suppliers as analytical references; 'weapons grade' in terms of purity. Comparing the active ingredient reference standards with their occurrences in gin samples allowed me to calculate how much 'active ingredients' make gins what they are. In theory, this would be proportional to the quantities of botanicals required to produce them. And if that held true, would it then be possible to produce an artificial product, a synthetic product?

I coined the term SynGyn. This gave me a way to separate this creative concoction in manufacturing terms, yet still maintain a name of sorts that paid homage to gin. Replacing the I in gin with a Y was a subtle way to embrace curiosity and pose the question 'Why?'

The stumbling block – which took me quite some time to resolve – was recognising that some flavour compounds were drawn from multiple sources. For instance, alpha pinene occurs in juniper berries and some other botanicals used in gin.

The notion of SynGyn soon met a speedy and timely death, which upon reflection was both pleasing and gratifying.

One of the best lessons learnt during this time was that there is often neither a right nor wrong answer when it comes to flavour compounds, nor the gin maker's choice of botanicals that produce them. There is only the best answer, the answer that meets the goals of any gin making adventure. From this fleeting experience it became clear; synthetic gin – SynGyn – was never destined to be the best answer.

Comparing gin making with culinary pursuits

Let's use an example from the culinary arts as an analogy: Aunt Mabel's scone recipe.

In simple terms, the recipe comprises a specific list of ingredients in specific quantities with a set of instructions that bring these ingredients to life. These historically important gems reflect heritage and legacy. They are often handwritten and shared among the next generation without using modern technology. Here's what they have in common:

A set of instructions that describe how to make gin is called an operating procedure. This information would exist in a single sheet of paper called a run-sheet. If there are variations to the run-sheet, these become unique operating procedures.

In other words, a set of ingredients and a recipe with instructions.

Like Aunt Mabel's scone recipe, each gin run-sheet refers to one product.

We can distinguish between Aunt Mabel's plain scones, date scones, cheese scones and herb scones by comparing their respective ingredient listings. The listings are not the same, their respective sets of instructions will be different, and the processes for making them will differ as well.

This makes perfect sense, because the end products are different. That said, they will share a common base recipe, or base, as depicted below.

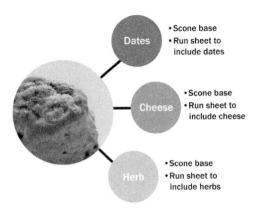

Date, cheese and herb scones

Gin making operating procedures are much the same. There will often be a set of common botanicals that can form diverse types of base. The run-sheet will include details concerning heat, time and duration. All bases must have the one thing that is characteristic of all gin: juniper. This is the standout botanical that distinguishes gin from all other alcoholic products.

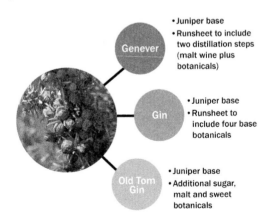

Genever, Gin and Old Tom Gin

GIN AND MUSIC

All gin may require juniper berries, but the berries on their own do not make gin. There are other botanicals that play a supporting role and which are vital to bringing all gin to life.

As is often the case with diverse art forms, there is a somewhat surprising connection between gin making and composing music.

Let's say you have a favourite three-piece band – Green Day or Cream come to mind. The former is a modern American rock band with its roots in British punk rock. The latter is an archetypal British rock band with its foundation in the American blues.

These three-piece bands comprise a drummer to set the pace, a bass player that adds depth to melody, and a lead guitarist that drives the lasting melody into your psyche. The voices of the band members help to bring all the musical components together, into a collective whole that is greater than the sum of the parts.

In gin, juniper sets the pace, the other botanicals bring depth and texture to the gin, their collective interactions with alcohol and water give all gin its enduring voice.

Consider extra botanicals as additional band members and you can see that the possibilities are endless. Not all band members gel together to produce the legacy they seek. Some band members click and produce musical memories for many people over long periods of time spanning generations. These musicians are noted for being prolific, to the extent that relatively few musicians produce most of the modern music that people listen to today. It's the 80:20 Pareto Rule[3] writ large for all to see.

The similarities with music come to the fore again. You will know first-hand that no two groups of musicians, playing the same general styles, produce the same thing. They are similar and deliver similar musical results that resonate with the listener, but they are distinctly different. This is a reasonable outcome to expect, given the range of creative capacity that all people have within themselves and their ability to express this through their craft.

To illustrate the point further, consider this. Did you know that Mozart, Bach, Beethoven and Tchaikovsky account for more than 80% of all classical music performed and played to effusive audiences all over the world? This is a remarkable statistic that shows how quality music from prolific composers can stand the test of time for centuries on end. Some of the finest gin producers forged their legacies in the eighteenth and nineteenth centuries, and still hold their own in this digital age: Gordon's Gin™ since 1769, Plymouth Gin™ since 1793, Beefeater since 1863.

---

3   https://en.wikipedia.org/wiki/Pareto_principle

A modern analogy of these eighteenth-century musical giants would be the Big Four of metal: Metallica, Megadeth, Slayer and Anthrax. Different expressions of the same musical genre, appealing to varying tastes in music and a broad demographic.

Gin making draws common ground in this regard. The gin you make is a product of executing the basics well, expressing the plain-language outcome you want to achieve and then sharing that outcome with interested people. You may find to your surprise that there are people with a hitherto unknown interest in gin that may fall in love with your product.

The creative and artistic elements of gin making, and music, cannot be understated; nor can the value of being prolific in pursuit of the right combination of botanicals that will bring your composition to life.

There is a gin for everyone, and your gin legacy could well become a popular preference.

Bases

Overview

In this section you will see how this building block puts the botanicals to work. Some have suggested to me that this is exactly how bands such as Fifth Harmony, One Direction or 5 Seconds of Summer start out. You may reserve judgement as you see fit.

This step also provides you with an introduction to the popular bases that the budding gin maker can use as starting points. Each base provides a kick-start to the gin making journey. This section will compare the bases and consider how different gin making approaches can produce an array of results for a multitude of tastes.

This section will use examples from French cuisine to describe five culinary bases and illustrate how mastering the preparation skills for these relates directly to useful skills for gin making.

Finally, a strong emphasis upon keeping accurate written records will round this out. In the digital age, there is a reliance upon software packages and sophisticated tools. Simplest is best. If you have any doubts, have a think about family favourite recipes that you would prepare on a regular basis. Chances are they are hand-written somewhere for future reference, and not in some digital form on the Cloud, or your smartphone or other digital device that may be at risk of a security breach. No nefarious digital hacker ever compromised the security of an analogue record handwritten in a book.

As an aside, when this book goes to print, Fifth Harmony comprises four members instead of five yet retains the same name. When I posed this observation to some, the best response I received was that their fan base has now become some de-facto fifth member. A clear example where less is more can have unexpected results.

Gin and cuisine

In French cuisine, there is a collection of sauces known as 'The Five Mother Sauces'. In summary, they are:

- Béchamel – milk and white roux
- Velouté – white stock (fish or chicken) and roux
- Espagnole – beef and brown roux
- Hollandaise – butter
- Red sauce – tomatoes

Any would-be chef or accomplished home cook needs to master these as part of their basic skills.

By doing so, you can then add additional ingredients to these bases and create new sauce expressions:[4]

- Béchamel – to make cheese sauce, Mornay sauce
- Velouté – to make herb sauce, white wine sauce

In gin making, there is a similar array of 'mother bases' that deliver the flavour characteristics many gin products have today. A selection of gin styles may be summarised in a similar fashion to the Mother Sauces as follows:

---

4   Other examples include Espagnole – to make mushroom sauce, Hollandaise – to make béarnaise sauces, Red sauce – to make puttanesca.

- Gin – juniper, additional botanicals, no distillation required

- Distilled Gin – juniper, additional botanicals / flavours permissible after distillation

- London Dry Gin – juniper, additional botanicals only permissible during distillation

- Genever Gin – juniper, malt wine

- Old Tom Gin – juniper, sweet botanicals, sugar, malt

Understanding how to combine the botanicals in the best way to make gin bases is a key building block in all gin product development.

Blending

In this section, you will learn about blending fundamentals, and the vital role that blending plays when producing gin. There are several tools and blending techniques that gin makers use that help control quality and lend themselves to consistent gin production. You will learn about the interesting effects that take place during the blending process. These become more important when making gin at scale, and so an introduction to this on a small scale provides the perfect platform to explore, apply and understand blending techniques.

Blending is a simple concept to understand and apply; take two or more items and mix them together. These items can be as diverse as metallic powders for use in fireworks; eggs and oil to make mayonnaise; sugar and egg whites to make meringues; mushrooms, beef and brown roux to make mushroom sauce; black and white paint to make grey paint; copper and tin to make bronze; angostura bitters and London Dry Gin to make Pink Gin.

However, whenever you're describing simple examples, this does not necessarily mean that delivering the result is an easy thing to do. On the contrary, there is still a level of skill, experience and know-how required to produce the results sought. Repetition, applying what you've learnt, and reinforcing what works are keys to success. A table like this drawn up in your A5 notebook is a simple tool to use and apply.[5]

What worked?

What worked?	What didn't work?
What shall I keep doing?	What shall I stop doing?

In gin making, blending is a manifold pursuit with an array of different techniques available. Each technique is nuanced with implications for the end-product result. This provides great opportunities for creative expression in a methodical, repeatable fashion.

---

5   This table is analogous to a SWOT analysis (strength, weaknesses, opportunities and threats) used in business strategy planning.

Blending different bases at different alcoholic strengths can provide amazing outcomes for the budding gin maker. However, be warned as in the absence of the basic tools described below, it will provide a relentless source of frustration; simple does not mean easy.

Here's an example. The ability to combine a fruity base with a spicy base, perhaps with hints of a floral or citrus base extends the range of outcomes, limited solely by the gin maker's imagination. Some of the ideas may be breathtaking, but unless you have the details recorded somewhere with easy access, it could become a lost opportunity with little chance of recovery. Disciplined record keeping is key.

In what may be a surprising insight for most people, the most challenging item to blend with is the seemingly simplest one of all: water.

Water is the dark horse in all gin making. It plays a role in gin testing, tasting and distillation. Its combination with alcohol produces a chemically and physically significant liquid blend called an azeotrope. A blend with a strange name, and even stranger characteristics.

Water boils at 100° Celsius, alcohol at 78.3° Celsius. Yet the azeotrope boils at 78.2° Celsius; a temperature that is lower than either of its components.

This 0.1° Celsius difference in temperature between alcohol and its blend with water is the unsung piece of magic that takes place in every still. The botanicals' exposure to boiling temperatures is tempered by the water content over the duration of the process. It acts like a chemical handbrake allowing the botanicals to interact intimately. This means that for a significant period, the temperature remains constant but more importantly at a temperature that is lower than the boiling points water and alcohol command individually. Understanding this principle assists gin distillers in making assessments about what to keep and what to set aside.

This scientific fact provides a solid pillar for the art of distillation. Put simply, it's the azeotrope that is vital in efforts to deliver the heart for all gin.

In closing, here is an interesting aside to consider from a seemingly unrelated phenomenon: icy roads.

Icy roads are a common, well-known occurrence during cold, winter conditions. One safety measure to reduce the amount of ice on these roads is the application of salt to their surface. This has the effect of reducing the freezing point of the ice. Adding salt to a liquid – such as the azeotrope – increases the liquid's boiling point; saltwater will do this. This is because the salt reduces the liquid molecule concentrations. These two effects – freezing point depression and boiling point elevation – can present interesting outcomes for gin making.

Blending with water – industrial scale

While kicking off my industry career as a wide-eyed twenty-something in 1980s New Zealand, little did I realise that my years of study in chemistry would become an entry point into the liquor industry, leading to a niche specialism in distilled products. I was fortunate to work with some of the industry's finest and learnt a tremendous amount. This was a consequence of relentless curiosity, interest beyond the job and working with great people. One of the more intriguing observations I made concerned something quite innocuous: water, and its uses in making gin.

There's water for general consumption, and then there's water that is good enough for gin making. The use of water in gin making occupies two distinct areas: water use for manufacturing, and water use for production and quality control.

Water for manufacturing is typically sourced from municipal supplies. Water for production and quality control, however, is the result of treating water for manufacturing, and repurposing it for specific applications. These specific applications may be broadly described as blending but tempered by how the operational scale differs in each case.

Blending with water – small scale

For this exercise, you will need several identical wine-glasses, water and a spirit measure commonly used by bartenders.

Let's explore the blending process by using a bottle of commercial gin that you may have handy in your burgeoning gin collection. After all, I have yet to meet a budding gin maker with a ginless bar.

Consider this next exercise your first excursion into quality control and testing. As this is a small-scale operation, it is a relatively straightforward process that will help broaden your set of basic skills. It is also a very interesting part of the gin making process that is often left unexplored.

The gins you have at your disposal from your bar provide the perfect start. Each one has its own taste and aroma characteristics to consider and for documenting in your A5 notebook.

- Add a shot of gin into a wine glass.

- Add a shot of water to the gin.

- Swirl it to mix the gin and water together.

- Take in the gin's aromas and record your observations.

- Take a sip of the gin; record the taste characteristics in plain language, describing what you experience at first taste, when you allow the gin to settle in your mouth, and the after taste when you swallow the gin.

- Repeat this exercise for say two or three gins in all.

You now have a set of observations for reference that describe your assessments of the gins at hand.

Cup your hands around the bottom of the glass near the stem, and you will likely sense warmth. This is what the addition of water to alcohol produces. Mixing alcohol and water together produces heat at a molecular level. The cause of this heat generation is due to a chemical principle called hydrogen bonding. Water has two hydrogen atoms in its structure, alcohol – also known as ethanol or ethyl alcohol – has six hydrogen atoms, including a hydroxy group with a feature called a dipole. The creation of hydrogen bonds between the hydroxy group and the hydrogen atoms in the water creates heat.

Making gin

This section will describe:

- A straightforward way to start making gin using a kit[6]

- The importance of diligent record keeping

- The magic ratios concept

- The connection between gin making and making music

- Creating your own gin kit

- The steps you need to develop your superpowers for taste and aroma (olfactory senses)

- Organoleptic testing

- An initial venture into quality control processes

- A universal starting base

Getting started – gin kits

There are several manufacturers that produce ready-to-make gin kits available for purchase online. Simply type the terms 'gin kit' into your favourite search engine.

Although there are divided opinions about these kits, they have a place and provide an important and

---

6　All gin enthusiasts reading this book will learn about botanicals, filtration and a very important process called steeping when ordering a gin kit. However, if you are so keen that the thought of ordering a kit and waiting for it to arrive is too much to bear, continue reading and then learn about making your own kit in the section entitled 'Creating your own base'.

invaluable educational experience. The kits typically comprise a set of botanicals, simple instructions and provide a no-fuss route to making gin.

Steeping botanicals

Steeping botanicals (clockwise from top left: grapefruit, mandarin, coriander seeds, angelica root, cardamom, juniper berries and fennel)

In simple terms, steeping botanicals means soaking them in a liquid for a specific period. Common examples include brewing tea or coffee. In this case steeping takes place in a water/alcohol solution of known strength.

Most do-it-yourself (DIY) gin making kits require a bottle of vodka. The kit instructions will ask the gin maker to steep the botanicals in vodka for say 24–72 hours or overnight, at room temperature.

Why vodka?

Vodka is a mixture of alcohol and water, which typically ranges in strength between 37%–40% ABV. More importantly, it is a ready-made source of alcohol that requires no effort to produce or manufacture. Simplicity in its finest form.

Once the steeping process is complete, you will then use a tea strainer or a funnel and filter to remove the botanicals and pour the gin into bottles of your choice.

Some kits will even provide you with a self-adhesive label for you to record the fruits of your labour.

However, the best part about the kits lies in the botanicals themselves.

When you receive your kit, make sure you have the A5 notebook handy and a pen. Write notes on the right-hand side pages of the notebook, leaving the left-hand side blank.

In this way, you can get into the habit of documenting what you do and using the blank left-hand side of the book for additional notes, observations, pictures and other commentary.

Identify each of the botanicals. Write these down in your notebook, perhaps consider drawing pictures of the botanicals as well. Touch and feel each botanical and write about the aromas and textures the botanicals present to you. Consider colour, size, shape, and any other description that comes to mind as you examine each botanical in turn. This will help you to develop a 'feel' for the botanicals, their earthiness and an appreciation for how so little can produce so much in a reasonably short period.

Collect the botanicals into piles: juniper in one pile, coriander in another pile and so forth.

Place each pile into a wine glass; gently wave your hand over each glass to waft the aromas of the botanicals. Breathe in their scent, try to describe what your senses are telling you, and write this down. Use simple language: piney, dirty, fresh, acrid; whatever takes to your mind immediately.

Next, pour out the largest pile of botanicals, weigh them, and note these measurements down in your notebook. From experience, creating a small table with the botanical names down the left-hand side and the weight of each one to the right makes the information easy to access and compare. Try to get into the habit of weighing the botanicals starting with the largest quantity first, and the lightest last. This is a useful habit to reinforce from the start.

Extend the table in your notebook to be have a column for each botanical. So, if you have five botanicals, have a table with five rows and five columns.

Once you've created the table, weighed out all the botanicals and matched the quantities against each botanical in turn, you will uncover magic in the numbers: magic ratios. See if you can figure out which base this table refers to.

Magic ratios

	Juniper	Coriander	Angelica	Cardamom	Citrus
Juniper	1				
Coriander		1			
Angelica			1		
Cardamom				1	
Citrus					1

Botanical quantities

Gin is a combination of many things that need to be in balance. This exercise immediately uncovers one of the simplest ways to gather insights into gin formulations. The botanicals themselves are important to include, but it's the combination with other botanicals that unlocks the magic that gin keeps hidden.

Compare the weight of juniper with the weight of coriander; angelica; cardamom; citrus, and so on until you have compared juniper with all the other botanicals.

Let's say you have 10 grams of juniper and 5 grams of coriander. This means that the ratio between the two botanicals is 2: 1; for every 2 grams of juniper, we need 1 gram of coriander.

Repeat this exercise for each botanical in turn, and you will find a pattern, a numerical pattern that is so remarkably simple yet holds the key to all gin botanicals. You are taking a trip back to a time when the first gin makers were discovering what they could do with the botanicals they had available, and the best way to balance their use. Some botanicals were scarce, subject to seasonal variation and demand, and as such were treated with great care.

Welcome to your first piece of gin making science. You have a set of botanicals, in known quantities, which you know will ultimately produce gin when you follow the instruction correctly.

Bringing that kit to life

You are now ready to follow the instructions and make your own gin. For most kits most of the time, the gin maker is in fact flavouring vodka with a selected array of botanicals. From a definition viewpoint, gin needs to have juniper berries in the finished product, so to that extent, the DIY kits satisfy this condition. You're on your way to making gin. More importantly, you are also recreating the ways and means that the first British gin makers used in the late seventeenth century. This is a step back in time, your first venture into gin's heritage, whose legacy is enjoyed worldwide.

Usually you will need to provide a bottle of vodka, a large jar with a lid, a filter funnel and filter paper such as those used in coffee making, and bottles to collect your finished product.

After a steeping period of between 24 and 72 hours, the resulting jar full of vodka and botanicals will look a little yellowish or straw coloured.

Using a filter and funnel will help remove the botanicals from the liquid and you'll be left with a juniper flavoured vodka.

The next step on your journey is to take some of this finished product, and put it into a freezer overnight. Observe and record what you see in your A5 notebook. This may surprise you at first glance so it's noteworthy. Is it clear or cloudy, coloured or neutral? What happens when the gin can stand at room temperature?

Last, but not least, taste your gin. Gin makers have an approach to the way they sample finished gin. Reducing the gin in strength to 20% or 23% ABV is a standard that has been in place for many years. For the budding gin maker, however, the following approach is the simplest and best one to take.

Pour equal portions of gin and water into a small wine glass, swirl and record what you observe. Did the temperature or colour change? What happened when you added the water? Cover the wineglass immediately with a saucer (or with a larger, upturned glass) and allow it to stand for a few minutes. What happens? Note down your observations.

Remove the cover from the wineglass, swirl the contents and gently take in the gin aromas. Did you notice anything about the side of the glass before you swirled the contents? Continue to apply your sense of relentless curiosity.

Your olfactory super powers: smell and taste

'Olfactory' is a description that refers to one's sense of smell. This, in turn, is closely related to your sense of taste, often called 'gustatory perception' or gustation. For ease of explanation, this book makes no distinction between smell and taste, preferring to bundle these up as your super power senses.

After the aroma assessment, there are three parts to gin tasting that follow:

1. Initial taste

2. Palate

3. Finish and aftertaste

An excellent habit to develop when you are first starting assessments – or if you find yourself having to make several assessments – is to use the voice recorder function on a mobile phone.

Document the key details in your A5 notebook before you start. Open the assessment with such details as your name, the date, time, and subject matter that you are investigating. Inexpensive transcription services such as Rev[7] are available to help you capture your observations as written text for your records and future reference. Speaking into a recorder for the first time can be a little daunting at first but as is the case with developing any new habit, it does get easier over time.

Otherwise, listening back to your observations and adding the key details to your A5 notebook is the most expedient approach to take, and one that will pay dividends in the longer term.

Tasting the gin

Let the gin play on your tongue for a moment and notice how the flavour affects various parts of your

---

7   https://rev.com

tongue in diverse ways. Did you like the first taste? How would you describe it in simple language?

Testing your palate

Swirl the gin in your mouth before swallowing. How would you describe the taste of the gin as you swirled it in your mouth? Describe the taste before you swallow the gin.

Record all observations you have made about the taste sensations you experienced.

Testing the finish and after taste

Describe the taste sensation you experience after you swallow the gin. Was it long and lingering? Was it spicy, sweet, earthy, fruity? Make notes about these observations in your A5 notebook. Again, use simple language that is easy to understand. By speaking a common language, you will be in position to bridge any gaps between the senses and any other individual's description of the same experience. This will also help you to describe what you are experiencing to other people.

The process of collecting information concerning gin aromas and the various taste sensations are collectively known as Organoleptic Tests. Gin makers conduct these on a regular basis as quality control checks for:

- Existing products

- Comparison with other products

- As controls for new products they may like to develop for commercial release

These exercises represent your first steps in developing your super power senses and applying simple quality control processes for your gin.

Industrial scale taste testing

My initial experiences with triangular taste testing at scale underwent further progress during my new product development role with a large Australian spirits company in the 1990s. In short, there are three samples to consider; two are identical and the third is a variation. These samples are placed into tasting glasses and allowed to stand, covered by a glass disc called a watch glass. A selection of people will then assess the three samples and select the one they think is different. Once they've made their selection, assessors record the volunteer testers' feedback concerning what they felt set a sample apart from the others. The larger the number of volunteers in the exercise, the more significant the result. The benefits of this type of test are its objectivity, simple set-up and results tally. It is a valuable tool for all budding gin makers to consider and a straightforward way to bring a sense of involvement and value-add into to your projects.

Your own gin kit

Given the ease with which a budding gin maker can create a product from a simple set of botanicals, it is possible to use the same approach, but using botanicals of your choice. After all, who wants to make everyone else's gin and merely succeed in being a lesser version of something else?

So long as you can find a source of juniper berries, your only limitation to what the gin may resemble is your imagination. Granted, imagination is something that people have in different degrees, but everyone has it lurking within themselves somewhere; it's a case of unleashing it on the unsuspecting public and seeing what happens.

The table 'Gin bases and botanical listings', which follows later in the chapter, illustrates a few options that you may want to experiment with. In Chapter Three there is a set of well known, tried and trusted botanical combinations that will provide you with a kick-start.

One major consideration as you become more expert lies with balancing different flavour types. Here are the five essentials for all gin making; they form the classic gin canon:

- Juniper berries are piney, with hints of camphor if you crack open the berry.

- Coriander seeds are mundane when dry but develop in alcohol.

- Angelica root is the dark lord. It has an earthy aroma, reminiscent of wet hessian sacks, yet its role in gin is very important.

- Cardamom is a great complement to juniper.

- A form of citrus, be it dried peel, whole fruits or fresh peel, brings a freshness and zest to the flavour as well.

These five botanicals contribute to a universal base, one that appears in many gin styles and whose variations live on today as gin legacies. They also form an important group of botanicals called a Gin canon. Differing ratios between each botanical helps all gin makers to distinguish between different canons. If there is a better place or reason to start with anything other than these five botanicals, I have yet to see it.

You will find that The Advanced Botanical Lexicon in Chapter Two of this book has an array of common botanicals and concise descriptions of their flavours. It will enable you to translate a clear flavour description into a series of botanical options. Each option has the potential to deliver the flavour you would like in your gin. In some cases, there are several options to consider so this allows you to experiment, and to compare the different nuances. Remember to note all your observations in your A5 workbook.

Magic gin ratios and music

Botanicals are compiled into various ratios that form bases for some of the most famous brands on the planet. In ways that are akin to pop music, the bases are available for the artist – or in our case, the budding gin maker – to take a known framework and apply their own signature to these.

Modern day musicians refer to this process as creating their own sound. In gin making, the same principle applies; hence there are so many brands of gin available. Despite that fact, most gins generally have the same set of base botanicals to begin with.

Like notes on a musical scale, the botanical notes you choose and the order in which you use them has an enormous influence on the outcome.

Get gin botanicals out of balance or out of sequence, and you'll end up with the musical equivalent of dud notes that grate instead of sounding great. No one pays good money to see a great musician or band play dud notes or sing off-key on more than one occasion.

Treat the botanicals poorly and you will deliver a finished product that leaves people flat and disappointed.

And here is where the value of a kit comes into its own. You may source your own supplies of the same botanicals for contrast and comparison. Keeping good records in your A5 notebook is key and will help you gain confidence with the science that makes gin making tick. The art will come soon enough but the key here is this: a DIY gin making kit is more than a straightforward way to make gin. It's an educational tool that will help you to learn and to apply simple principles with ease.

These principles are known to work if you follow a set of simple instructions; now you can apply them to your own gin making efforts from here on in with confidence.

Describing gin

Gin makers similarly follow a simple structure when describing their products.

- Origin and references to heritage

- Process followed

- Botanicals in use

- Flavour notes to expect

The pitch model that most gin distillers use is one that is simple to describe and easy to understand. Casual consumers and enthusiasts alike will gain insights, a view of the gin maker's authority and an indication of what to expect from the product.

Here are some notable examples to consider when trying to describe the gin you would like to create.

Australian Christmas Gin™ 2018:

> 'The result smells like gin and tastes like Christmas. Sip neat, pour over your pudding or make a cracking Martinez.'[8]

The West Winds Sabre Gin™:

> 'The Sabre is a gin lover's gin with a strong undercurrent of citrus, weaving through 12 spices and botanicals, including juniper, lemon myrtle, lime peel, and wattle seed.'[9]

Here's another terrific example of a very popular and well-crafted gin from Chase Distillery in the UK:

> 'Made from our own distilled spirit that is grown, fermented, and distilled on our family farm deep in the middle of England, we have selected ten of the finest botanicals to ensure the driest gin possible. (As well as juniper berries, we have used juniper buds.)'[10]

For Lilly Pilly Gin™, from the Tamborine Mountain Distillery®:

8   www.fourpillarsgin.com.au/buying/australian-christmas-gin
9   https://thewestwindsgin.com
10 https://chasedistillery.co.uk

'Tamborine Mountain Distillery is Australia's smallest operating pot still distillery, world renowned for their use of native flora to handcraft a unique elixir. It is the essence of the Australian landscape.)'[11]

Here's an example taken from the Chatham Islands, located east of New Zealand's South Island where Black Robin Gin™ is distilled:

'Black Robin Gin combines traditional exotic botanicals with native New Zealand Horopito, one of the world's most ancient flowering plants. The spicy citrus flavour is exceptionally delicate and balanced, creating a distinctive mellow texture with a refreshing unique flagrance and an elegant and refined finish.'[12]

Rogue Society (now known as Scapegrace™) Premium Dry Gin:

'Twelve hand selected wild botanicals, artesian waters from New Zealand's Southern Alps, relentlessly sourced, artistically combined.'[13]

Cousin Vera's Gin™, a collaboration between Four Pillars Gin of Australia and Santamanía Destileria

---

11 https://tamborinemountaindistillery.com/product/Lilly-Pilly-Gin
12 https://blackrobingin.co.nz
13 www.scapegracegin.com

Urbana from Spain, is a fabulous example of botanical grouping using clear, precise language:

'Spanish botanicals: Almond, white pepper, coriander seed;

Australian botanicals: lemon myrtle, olive leaf, Tasmanian pepper leaf, coriander, orange peel.'[14]

If you can be clear and precise in your descriptions, this will help you visualise the outcome that you seek and help others 'get' what you are about.

A universal gin base

This section has a table listing five initial gin bases to try as a first practical step. Each of the bases will have additional suggestions to consider. But in the spirit of creativity and free-spiritedness, use or discard these suggestions as you see fit, but only after you've made and tried a base or two yourself. There are benefits in making each gin base, assessing each one in turn, record-ing your observations and reflecting upon what you've discovered. As you move through this section, you will discover that the botanical listings and quantities are by design and will present you with a more comprehen-sive understanding of the botanicals and bases.

This will then allow you to apply the third B – Blending – and unleash an exciting world of creativity at your

---

14 www.fourpillarsgin.com.au/distilling/our-first-distiller-series

fingertips. You can also determine and record what did or did not work, what to continue or stop.

Creating your own base

Try this for size. For every 10 grams of juniper try 5 grams of coriander, 1 gram of angelica, a tenth of a gram of peel.

Here is a simplified list of taste sensations you can produce, using certain botanicals. This is a good set of bases to keep in your A5 notebook for easy reference. It can be easy to get carried away. Therefore, consider no more than 6–10 botanicals in any gin you intend to produce at the start of your journey. Remember the story earlier about Fifth Dimension and make 'less is more' your mantra.

- Almond – sweet
- Angelica seed – earthy, hessian sacks; key to binding botanical flavours together
- Cardamom – spicy, citrus flavours; I feel that green pods are more delicate than black pods
- Cassia bark – cinnamon
- Cinnamon – sweet
- Ginger root – spicy
- Grains of paradise – superb botanical, hot, spicy, peppery

- Grapefruit – clean citrus

- Nutmeg – spicy sweet

- Cubeb berries – peppery

- Camomile – floral

Remember the exercise we went through with the gin kit? Well now is the time to shine, by applying what you've learnt and to take the first tentative steps toward expressing gin your way.

Here is a table of various gin bases and botanical listings to try for your own product developments. The common component – in addition to juniper – is bottled vodka, used 200ml at a time. This gives you an opportunity to try these products out at a small scale and make assessments as you see fit. Some of the Base Groupings highlight some other botanicals that are worth experimenting with, such as Grains of Paradise, rosemary and bitter orange.

Again, make sure that you have your A5 note-book handy to write these down, and record your observations.

As a broad hint and strong recommendation, invest a fair amount of energy in exploring Base II.

This will become more apparent as the book pro-gresses, so consider yourself told.

Gin bases and botanical listings

To make 200ml of Gin	Botanical	Base I	Base II	Base III	Base IV	Base V
Base Groupings	Juniper (grams)	10.0	12.0	9.0	5.0	10.0
	Coriander (grams)	4.0	3.0	4.0	5.0	5.0
	Angelica (grams)			1.0		2.0
	Green Cardamom pods uncrushed (grams)				8.0	
	Green Cardamom pods crushed (grams)					1.0
	Bitter orange (grams)					
	Grapefruit pieces					6.0
	Lemon rind (grams)		3.0	1.0	1.0	
	Lemon pieces		3.0			3.0
	Limes (grams)					

Continued

59

To make 200ml of Gin	Botanical	Base I	Base II	Base III	Base IV	Base V
Bass Notes	Orange strips	1.0	3.0	1.0	1.0	6.0
	Liquorice Root sticks			1.0	1.0	
	Orris root (grams)					
	Cassia (grams)					1.0
	Fennel (grams)		1.0			1.0
Treble Notes	Allspice (grams)	2.0	1.0			
	Bay leaf (no. of leaves)	1.0				
	Cloves (grams)		2.0			2.0
	Grains of paradise (grams)					
	Peppercorns (grams)	1.0				
	Rosemary sprig					

The best part about this type of record keeping is that it provides an easy reference to access for future work. They also provide a great journal that will help you chronicle your own journey through the gin firmament. This will allow time to reflect on what worked, and what was an opportunity for improvement. Remember to think about and note what you felt worked well and what did not. By developing this repeatable approach, you will reinforce a useful habit that will help you to document and capture your experiences in your own words.

These are variations on a few of the many gin bases that I've collected over the years spent with gin consumers, commercial manufacturers and gin enthusiasts the world over. These are merely a guide and provide you with an insight into the starting points that are common for each, and the creative, supportive parts that drive the gin's development overall.

Note that the different bases have different quantities of juniper and coriander. This is no accident. The reasoning for this is to help understand the impact these two key botanicals have upon the final product.

For example, Base I consists of 10:4 juniper to coriander, Base IV has 1:1 juniper to coriander, but with additional cardamom to complement the juniper.

Base II has 12:3 juniper to coriander, to complement a host of citrus botanicals.

Bases III and V include angelica, which brings an earthiness to the gin and binds the other botanicals together.

Here is the magic ratio table for Base III. In your A5 workbook transcribe something like this table and repeat the exercise for the other bases. By putting your sensory super powers to use and applying some simple mathematics you will start to make connections between the art and science of gin making.

Magic ratio table for Base III

	Juniper	Coriander	Angelica	Cardamom	Citrus
Juniper	-	4/9	1/9	-	2/9
Coriander	9/4	-	1/4	-	2/4
Angelica	9/1	4/1	-	-	2/1
Cardamom	-	-	-	-	-
Citrus	9/2	4/2	1/2	-	-

Note too that that the ratios of juniper to coriander are similar, with similar arrays of citrus. The key differences between the two, however, lies with the inclusion of treble and bass notes to complement the botanicals in Base V.

The value-added outcome with this approach lies in the variations between each gin type and their small-scale, inexpensive production. If you start making each gin base at the same time, you will quickly determine which one you like best within a 24-hour period.

To do this, the quantities of botanicals are small, and the costliest outlay will be for two bottles of vodka. The quantities of finished gin are such that you can use empty jars with lids, or unused, clean bottles with screwcaps to cover the product while steeping takes place. It also means that you if choose to rule out a gin from further work, then the write-off cost is minor to do so.

That said, there is value in retaining the gins that you did not like first up for three reasons:

1. Allow the flavours to develop over time.

2. The number of times I have dismissed a gin formulation, only to revisit it later and review my position is one of the greatest lessons to learn. It also demonstrates how invaluable the documentation process for this work can be, and one that I would strongly recommend that every budding gin maker adhere to wholeheartedly.

3. Keep the gin formulations handy as standards when the bases undergo additional treatment described in Chapter Two Distillation. We can compare the effects between 'steeped' gin and 'distilled' gin. It's an advanced technique and exciting to use. It will accelerate learning, significantly advance your gin making skills, and produce gin at a far faster rate than that prescribed by a kit.

The distilling processes are the cornerstone of traditional and commercial gin operations; this work will prove to be an invaluable step in the skills development process.

Preparation for Chapter Two – Distillation

Objective reasoning

One of the most valuable skills everyone can learn is to harness the ability to objectively reason. This helps distillers, artisans and people from all walks of life enormously, when solving a diverse array of problems. This technique is particularly useful if the outcome is uncertain, risky or challenging. The creative arts lend themselves to these types of challenges, where the merging of expression and tangibility can be difficult to describe as an outcome. Moreover, describing the outcome in plain language merely compounds this challenge but is key for buy-in. After all, how else will anyone 'get' what you're about if your message or vision are unclear?

There are five tools of the trade which I know lead to great results. It takes time, patience and practice but once proficient in their use your problem-solving capability and capacity will sky-rocket.

Example Question: I am convinced that my gin needs a citrus note that is easy to obtain all year round. What are the best options?

1. Sweet Navel oranges from California

2. Pomeloes from Spain

3. Grapefruit from the local farmer

4. Limes from my garden

Develop clarity

Be clear about the outcome you are looking for – with Step 1 in the D.I.S.T.I.L. process, the intent is to make decisions. The best way to get clarity is to think about a key question to answer. Write down a set of answers and choose one. Take confidence in the fact that there is neither a right nor wrong answer; there is only the best answer.

Gather information

You now have the best answer; go wild online and gather as much information as you can.

With Step 2 in the D.I.S.T.I.L. process, the key to success lies in investigations.

Here is the catch. Gather information that is both supportive and challenging to your answer. Make a list of these viewpoints spanning two pages of your A5 notebook. Put a supportive statement on the left, and then a challenging statement on the right. Then, and only then, write another supportive statement on the left, and another challenging statement on the right; repeat the exercise. Avoid the temptation – which in fairness is one we've all learnt from schooling – to write all of the supportive statements and then all of the challenging statements. You will soon see the benefits of this approach and gain a different perspective.

Apply information

You will find yourself running out of supportive statements or challenging statements at some point. If you find that you can keep the left- or right-hand side going, then continue until you have exhausted all thoughts. For example:

- If the list of statements on the left is longer than the right then the benefits outweigh the cost, meaning you have found the best answer.

- If the number of statements on the right is larger than the left then the cost outweighs the benefits, and it's time to think again.

With Step 3 in the D.I.S.T.I.L. process, the sampling technique can apply here as well. The subject is a statement but one that is ready for scrutiny and assessment.

This principle is no different to seeking alternative answers to the 'gin question' described earlier.

Consider implications

Once you've substantiated the merits of the answer, you will now need to understand what this means. A table like this drawn up in your A5 notebook can be a useful way to visualise this step. Make notes concerning the pros and cons for each option. It is quite possible that an alternative may come into play based upon a new viewpoint.

Steps 4 and 5 in the D.I.S.T.I.L. process are wrapped up in this concept as well.

1. Sweet Navel oranges from California

2. Pomeloes from Spain

3. Grapefruit from the local farmer

4. Limes from my garden

Consider other viewpoints

No single person can claim to be an expert in all things, always. It makes sense then to garner input from peers, other experienced people or experts you know in the field. This is a decision in and of itself that will also need to stand up to objective reasoning.

Step 6 in the D.I.S.T.I.L. process – Launch – can refer to a decision to act and proceed as intended.

Implications

Implications for:	Sweet Naval	Pomeloes	Grapefruit	Limes
Cost				
Quality				
Reliable supply				
Time to supply				
Freight cost				
Insurances				
Storage				
Risk of spoilage				
Reputation				

Closing remarks

Sharpening your skills in this area will provide you with a structured framework and confidence in your abilities to craft the right questions, some options and an approach to backing up your answer. This approach will complement the D.I.S.T.I.L. process, meaning that your skills will grow over time, as will your ability to apply them.

CHAPTER TWO

Distillation

Spirits distillation has a long history dating back to the ancient Greeks. The following timeline outlines its journey since 1100 CBE.

- 1100 – Middle Eastern distillers

- 1150 – Monks and Alchemists

- 1300 – Juniper Medicines

- 1500 – European distilling

- 1550 – Juniper distillates

- 1585 – Dutch Courage

- 1600 – Grain spirits

- 1720 – Mother's ruin

- 1730 – London awash with Gin

- 1800 – Gin goes industrial scale

For the purposes of this book, the focus will be on more recent times and the specific distillation technique used to make gin.

The 3Bs

Recap

In Chapter One of this book you learnt about seventeenth-century gin making and the building blocks that are its cornerstone: botanicals, bases and blending. There were some analogies drawn from music and cuisine to provide additional context and common ground concerning the use of building blocks in different vocations. Chapter One also described some additional nuances about the 3Bs ranging from steeping, blending with water, and heat from hydrogen bonding.

Chapter Two will reinforce the principles of the 3Bs by applying them to the D.I.S.T.I.L. process model for making distilled gin.

Process review

You will recall from Chapter One that there were instructions to make gin using vodka and an array of botanicals as complements to the juniper that all gin requires. The gins may have come from a pre-ordered kit or from the listings in the Bases section of the 3Bs' description.

You have made notes about this process, collected observations and insights concerning the aroma, taste, palate and finish for each of the gins you attempted to make.

Here is the key insight from those activities.

The products you have made to date are gins, so from that viewpoint you can say that you've satisfied the requirements for gin making. However, they play another role in a different process; the D.I.S.T.I.L. process. The same gin base formulations used in Chapter One are called a Still Charge in Chapter Two.

In other words, a still charge comprises the combination of alcohol, water and botanicals used to make gin. In Chapter One you made gin via steeping. Chapter Two will supercharge the gin making process by using a copper still.

Distilled Gin requires alcohol, water, botanicals and a still. The 3Bs provide all these materials except the still. The water that the still charge needs is in fact contained in the vodka used for the initial gin making exercises described in Chapter One.

You will now bring the 3Bs into play by using the same gin bases prepared earlier, for additional treatment in a copper still but the differences now will be in both scale and speed. The gins in Chapter One occupy about 200ml of product at the strength of the vodka used. For the small-scale works set for Chapter Two, a good rule of thumb is to limit the still charge size to range between 60–75% of the copper still capacity.

Distilled gin – Fundamentals

From Chapter One you now know that making gin is more than basic science. It is also an art, an art that distillers have handed down from generation to generation. Distillation concerns treating a set of botanicals, in an alcohol-water solution. Distillers do this by applying and controlling heat, following instructions, managing the use of time, sampling, adjusting and reflecting on their progress along the way. Regular assessments will compel them to maintain their course of action, or to make corrections along the way. In many ways, running a distillation process to produce gin resembles a commercial airline flight. There is a significant level of preparation before boarding, a flurry of activity from the pilot to get the aircraft into the air followed by a lengthy period of relative calm. The end of a gin production run resembles a pilot's preparation for landing the aircraft safely with all on board. Safety, quality and restraint are key characteristics that all distillers need possess.

Finishing off a gin production run is as important as starting off on the right footing.

For those of you who experience the miracle of modern air travel, people often remark that the most annoying part is the number of on-flight announcements that take place in the last 20–30 minutes when you're trying to see out the conclusion of a riveting movie or other entertainment. For others, it's the inability to have 'one more drink for the road' as the cabin crew prepare for landing, cross check and belting themselves up.

Distilled gin and cuisine

In Chapter One I compared gin making with cuisine.

The biggest difference between distilled gin making and cuisine concerns the steps that a distiller takes next. Unlike a chef or home cook, a distiller's attention does not focus on what people can see, but rather what people *do not see*.

Let's say you were to follow a soup recipe, one that was handed down to you by your parents, grandparents or some other significant figure from your life; it is the content of the pot that will encourage an emotional response. This may be positive, negative or somewhere in between.

Families can be playfully brutal in this regard, suggesting that you may need more practice to improve on your latest effort. Interestingly these same people are more than willing to assist with your quest for improvement, suggesting that there are ulterior motives for their critiques.

In other words, any excuse for a meal that they needn't cook themselves under the guise of constructive feedback.

When you serve your soup, made with such care and attention, there are few more satisfying achievements to share. The spirit of sociability is there for all to see, and all being well, will not result in some form of family warfare; differences of opinion may escalate all out of proportion. After all, traditions and standards need to be upheld. But what does this have to do with distilling? And more importantly, what does this have to do with making gin? Well, the difference between making soup and making gin lies in the process itself.

When you are making soup, and cover it with a transparent glass lid, you will see some interesting things. However, they are only interesting if you are prepared to look and know what to look for. That is the skill, that is art, but it is also basic science.

Over time, while the soup is cooking, steam will form in the pot, and rise. This steam will only rise to a point no higher than the height of the pot, until it runs into

the lid. You may have taken no interest in this whatsoever in the past, but now is the time to pay attention.

The steam will start producing droplets, through a
process is called condensation. This is the result of the
steam temperature exceeding the outside temperature
of the lid.

When a distiller sees this, their eyes light up with
anticipation and excitement.

A distiller would look interested in the array of soup
ingredients, so lovingly selected and cooking in the
pot to produce grandpa's soup, but for assorted
reasons.

The distiller is interested in the flavours and nuances
that the pot contents produce in the *steam*.

That's the difference and it's an important one.
Anyone can see the soup, bubbling away, and occa-
sionally causing the pot lid to bounce when the heat
produces steam at a rate that forces the lid to rattle,
causing that wonderful clattering sound of food on
the way.

A distiller, however, sees goodness and wonderful flavour escaping from their grasp, and rues this fact.

But what would a distiller do? Get a taller pot perhaps? Or maybe a better lid with something that can

catch the droplets as the steam condenses. These are all interesting ideas, simple to describe, and simple to test.

The best answer is a combination of these two ideas. Allow the steam to travel higher. We don't need a bigger pot for that, maybe a pipe on top of the pot so that all the steam channels its way upward.

But what happens when it gets to the top of the pipe? Won't it fall back into the pot?

Yes, but only if the pipe is straight. If you put a bend in the top of the pipe, the steam has a choice; it can fall back into the pot, or if it is energetic and strong enough it can make its way toward the bend.

But if it swerves into the bend, what happens next?

Well, that's the portion of the steam that the distiller is interested in collecting. If the distiller conjures up a way to cool the steam, then a liquid will form that is rich with flavour.

But how long will this take?

That's the combination of art and skill that you as a reader will understand from this book.

It should come as no surprise to you then that based on this simple analogy, most gin making stills in use today are called Pot Stills. They comprise large spherical copper pots atop a heat source, with a pipe – called a column – affixed to the top of the pot. There is a bent section of pipe at the top of the column called a lyne arm. A metal jacket – called a condenser – surrounds the lyne arm with water, causing any vapour in this part of the still to condense into liquid. At the base of the lyne arm is a vessel that collects the droplets called the distillate.

All flavour-rich steam that travels up the column and returns to the pot follows a process called reflux. A distiller can control the rate of reflux by adjusting the temperature of the heat source over time. The benefits of reflux lie in producing richer deeper flavours, like simmering a pot of soup, creating a rich sauce or stock for other dishes.

The downside to reflux is that the distiller will not collect any of the flavour-rich droplets, as none of the steam will rise through the column. This in turn means that the steam will not condense into droplets that the distiller intends to collect.

From this description, it's easy to see that the art and science of distillation is a balancing act. One where we want to produce lots of flavour for a hearty product during reflux, but in such a way that we can also unlock the flavours that are bubbling forth following a condensation process... and copper holds the key.

Distilled gin and music

Gin making is a spiritual experience in more ways than one. As gin makers, we have a tradition to uphold that was forged by the Dutch, reinforced by British solders fighting arm in arm with them, and influenced by the whims of a hitherto unheard of seventeenth century Dutch monarch.

Chapter One described a connection between gin making and making music. This connection referred to the musical world and its equivalents in the gin making world; the use of classical examples in both expressions described common ground.

What follows is a personal connection between my own musical journey and making gin. The result was obtaining an insight that I never fully appreciated until my gin making career began. In this interlude, I describe my late start to learning music, connections I made with some of those giants of the classical music era and the notion of a canon. Little did I realise at the time that the term canon describes the enduring, artistic connection between two completely disparate vocations; classical music and classically made gin.

A CLASSICAL INTERLUDE

Some years ago, I made a late start to learning the piano. The instrument I had at my home was a rickety old German upright, a common sight in many homes at the time. This instrument also had lots in common with its counterparts in these other homes: faded ivory keys, a few dud notes and a sustain pedal that refused to co-operate during home-based recitals. I use the term recital in its broadest possible sense as no doubt the audiences at the time were likely subjected to an aural ordeal rather than any Ode to Joy. I was fortunate to have a terrific piano teacher, patient, methodical and supportive of my efforts. As a late starter, I found that I could pick up new concepts quickly and reinforce them as well. There's something to be said for taking on a new pursuit at a more mature age, than at a time when you're learning to read, write, and listen to a stranger all day every day with a bunch of equally bewildered children at the start of a ten- to twelve-year journey in the education system.

My teacher's approach meant that I could focus on the basics of musical structure, expression, documentation and preparation for each subsequent lesson.

There was a turning point I can recall when a certain type of music resonated strongly with me. It came from the baroque era and is variously referred to as counterpoint or contrapuntal music. In simple terms, there are rules that govern how the various note structures blend together and complement each other. Some parts are independent, some combine to form harmonies. There was a describable science to the music that I had not considered before. I was hooked by the concept. It was the clearest example I had seen which brought the old saying that 'less is more' well and truly front and centre.

Canons

My next stop on the musical journey led to canons. I took an interest in works by Mozart and JS Bach, all giants of the musical firmament in the mid to late eighteenth century Europe. I practised like a man possessed. There was something deeply satisfying about its simplicity, the range of emotions it would stir, and its impact; from quiet reflection to pomp and grandeur. Bringing to life a simple set of notes on a page, seemingly unremarkable at first sight, proved to be one of the greatest lessons I would learn. I began to explore other works with an interest in a few well-known German and Austrian composers.

Fast forward to today, and you now know from Chapter One, that:

- A gin canon comprises five key botanicals united to produce a range of gin expressions
- Gin making unites art and science in predictable ways

There are certain structures or rules that apply to gin making, that have common ground with pursuits as diverse as the culinary arts or classical music. Each of these pursuits are steeped in heritage and guardianship; the legacy of those that have gone before us. I had no idea at the time just how important a part this would play until I entered the workforce three years later as an assistant distiller, my first job which was to encapsulate heritage, guardianship and legacy.

D.I.S.T.I.L. – Process overview for making distilled gin

Now that you have an insight into gin's colourful past, and its role in the present, we can have a look at what a gin making future would resemble with you at the helm.

This is a major difference to when I – and countless others before me – became involved in gin making in 1980s New Zealand. Back then, and indeed in the years prior, the art and craft of distilling was shrouded by a veil of secrecy and intrigue that James Bond would be proud of. The arrival of the internet has changed all of that, and so we no longer live in an age where information is king.

Success in a volatile, uncertain, chaotic and ambiguous (VUCA) world is driving greater collaboration between parties sharing a common sense of purpose. The barriers to entry are lower today, and there has never been a more exciting time to pursue a passion such as gin making, than right now.

You will recall from the overview of the 3Bs, gin making comprises a set of building blocks starting with botanicals to form a base. An array of additional botanicals creates flavour, depth and layers. Magic happens as the base and botanicals work together, creating a raw energy. A distiller's skill lies in directing these energies safely, with care and restraint.

The next part of the gin making journey replicates the same technological change that took place in eighteenth century London; the use of copper stills to accelerate the production of gin and improve its quality.

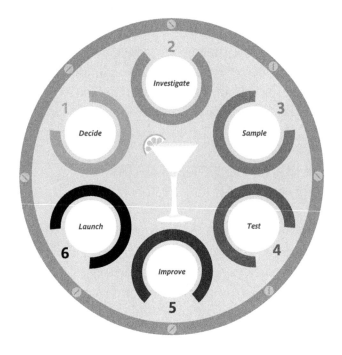

Decide, investigate, sample, test, improve and launch

Putting the 3Bs to work

The D.I.S.T.I.L. process refers to the six steps to consider when producing a new product. This approach is applicable to other distilling operations, but the focus here will solely be upon creating gin. Coupled with the 3Bs, the following sections illustrate the complete and remarkable solution for new gin product development.

Decide

Step 1 concerns decision-making; specifically deciding which characteristics you would like in your gin.

It doesn't have to be crystal clear or brilliantly conceived. It merely needs a clear description in plain language that is easy to understand. While you are thinking this through, avoid getting caught up by indecision or trying to find the right words. Sometimes it's a feeling, or an image as opposed to a definitive statement. For instance, it may be something along the lines of 'like one of the classic gins but with more fruit'.

Have a think about the fruit you have in mind. Maybe it's peaches, or grapefruit; maybe it's plums or something more exotic like a lychee or rambutan. You are limited solely by your imagination. Try to create a time to trigger thought processes in your mind and set yourself up to be in the 'zone' for creative thinking.

Turn off the TV, find a quiet space, turn on some music; do all the things that help you to think through what the final gin product would resemble.

It's a case of you deciding what the best answer is for you.

Whatever the answer is, using the Botanicals and Bases from the 3Bs will help make this determination and help to get you started.

Investigate

Step 2 of the D.I.S.T.I.L. process concerns Investigating if there is a similar gin to the one you've decided to create.

This is a chance to unleash your inner sleuth, or detective. Maybe there is a gin out there with similar characteristics to the one you would like to make. Online searches can help with this step.

Given the range of gins available there is a good chance of this happening. Perhaps friends and family have gins that you may not have considered or seen before; don't let this stop you from investigating.

Here's why.

Recall the analogy in Chapter One about the two different three-piece bands. The fact that the instruments are the same does not mean that the music they produce is identical.

The capacity for creative discovery is limitless so take the opportunity to investigate if similar gin ideas exist and consider how your gin would be better. After all, if it's your gin, it needs to be different and express your own considered intentions.

Sample

Step 3 of the D.I.S.T.I.L. process concerns sampling other gins.

In this step, you will try a range of gin products to help support the Step 2 – Investigate part of the process. In this step, you have a chance to put your olfactory senses to the test in ways described in Chapter One. Then you can refine what you would like your gin's characteristics to resemble.

Once you've found examples of the gins that interest you, you can consider purchasing them for sampling purposes.

Consider this step as a form of collecting, skill development and intelligence gathering MI5-style. There are a range of gins available on the market in any given part of the world. With the rapid adoption of online shopping, it is now possible to order any gin, from anywhere, at any time.

Step 2 and Step 3 complement each other. The fact that you may have discovered a gin of interest does not necessarily mean that you will purchase it. It is however a good option to keep in mind as there is no such thing as on oversized gin collection.

Be aware though that some products may attract additional charges when they arrive from overseas. Most vendors state this possibility up front, but it is best to be prepared; the charges may be as much as the product purchase itself.

Test

Step 4 of the D.I.S.T.I.L. process concerns testing your gin and comparing it with other gins.

As glamorous as this step in the D.I.S.T.I.L. process may sound, take it from distillers the world over; this is very draining and can be particularly frustrating work. The requirements are physically, mentally and emotionally demanding, requiring patience and perseverance. It's physically demanding because your olfactory senses – your superpowers from Chapter One – can overload very quickly, leading to physical exhaustion. This in turn means it will take a long time to recover before you can resume testing again. It is mentally demanding because you are comparing different versions of your gin product and need to make objective assessments between each.

It is emotionally demanding because you may think the changes you have made to a product provide the outcome that you seek. When you objectively determine that this is not the case, the emotional let-down can be tough to manage.

It requires patience and perseverance because this tried and trusted testing approach requires that you change the quantity of one botanical at a time.

The tasting glass can make a difference too. However, context is everything. There are glasses made for professional tasters and distillers whose design fits the job function. Once a gin becomes comingled with another source of flavour however, then the glassware in use makes no discernible difference.

All in all, it's enough to drive you to drink.

Improve

Step 5 of the D.I.S.T.I.L. process concerns making improvements to your gin.

This step is crucial and can consume as much time as Step 4 – Testing.

There are ways and means to link Steps 4 and 5 to help accelerate the completion of these steps collectively.

When you finally have what you think is the best answer to your gin decision, you've recovered from your testing-related hangover and the emotional let-downs that go together with Step 4, now is the time to consider improvements to the product. This means considering four elements that will put your sensory super powers to the test.

1. Aroma – half fill a wineglass with your gin, wave your hand over the glass and take in the aromas

2. Initial taste – describe the initial taste sensation you experience

3. Palate – describe the feeling you experience when you hold the gin in your mouth

4. After taste – swallow or discard the gin, and describe the experience

As part of the improvement process, you may also investigate how your gin stands up under three stress conditions:

1. Neat or neat over ice

2. Mixed with tonic

3. Mixed in a cocktail, eg:

    – Martini

    – Negroni

COCKTAILS

The Martini

The creative capacity that people have cannot be overstated. Armed with limited resources, imagination and a 'less is more' attitude, the evolution of the martini and its variations is a wonderful story. The following table illustrates how the composition of various martinis differ.

Martinis

Martini name	Parts Gin	Parts Dry Vermouth	Parts Sweet Vermouth	Parts 'other'	Garnish
Dry Martini	6	1	-	-	Seedless olive
Dirty Martini[17]	5	1	-	1 part olive brine	Seedless olive
Perfect Martini[18]	6	½	½		Seedless olive
Montgomery[19]	8	½	-	dash orange bitters	Orange zest

15 Dirty martinis are best made using boozy or barrel aged gins such as Dirty June or McI Ienry's Navy Strength.
16 https://thespruceeats.com/perfect-martini-recipe-759777
17 Difford's Guide for discerning drinkers https://diffordsguide.com

The negroni – 1919, Florence, Italy

Campari defines this cocktail as a Negroni[18]:

- 1 part amaro
- 1 part gin, London dry style
- 1 part sweet red vermouth, nothing fancy here

The key to this classic cocktail is to build it. Use a gin which balances the bitter orange and herbal amaro characteristics and harmonises with the sweet vermouth.

Pour the ingredients – in the order above – into an old-fashioned glass or tumbler. Fill the glass with ice. Stir the cocktail by pushing the ice into the alcoholic mixture. Garnish with an orange wheel.

Launch

Step 6 of the D.I.S.T.I.L. process is launching your product.

Congratulations! You've now completed the five steps required to produce a gin product that is one of your own making. The Launch step is when you decide who will receive your product and when. You may launch a quantity of gin for a special occasion; it may be solely for your own consumption; or it may have commercial viability, where you could launch a venture yourself, or enter a partnership with an expert.

18 https://campari.com/our-cocktails%23negroni

In Chapter Four you can find a scorecard that will help you decide at any time if your interest in gin warrants a leap into a commercial arrangement. It comes down to who you will expect to receive your product and when.

Decisions of this nature are about considering the following two-fold question and figuring out what the best answer is for you. Over time, as circumstances change, and opportunities present themselves, asking this two-fold question at a different time will likely yield a different answer.

What's the right Launch decision for me right now?	
Friends and Family – Hobby	Joint Venture
Solo – Hobby	Solopreneur

Commercial Launch	
No	Yes

Options

What is the best launch decision for me right now?

Distillers in seventeenth century London were the fortunate recipients of government support for a new, popular and profitable business. It's fair to say that the whole concept of Launch did result in production and consumption levels scaling stratospheric heights; which leads me to a spot of history, subtly noted in the timeline at the start of Chapter Two.

WHY WAS GIN REFERRED TO AS 'MOTHER'S RUIN'?

In seventeenth century London many factors conspired to a massive overproduction of gin, and its consumption by the masses. It is fair to say that the population was in the grips of a legally sanctioned drug epidemic. The reasons are manifold but here are a few:

- Gin was safer to drink than the local water supply
- Gin was NOT subject to taxation
- There were few barriers to entry for new-start distilling operations to make their mark
- Gin consumption provided an escape for many people enduring the hardships of seventeenth-century life

The specific references to mothers and women in general evoke a mixture of both shock and sadness in equal measure:

- Gin consumption was looked upon as being contraceptive in nature.

- The claims that gin allegedly possessed medicinal benefits encouraged women to drink with men on an equal footing. Sadly, one of the consequences of this practice was a rise in promiscuity for both men and women and the poor decision-making that often accompanied this behaviour.

- Some believed that a 'cure' for pregnancy was a bottle of gin and a hot bath. If this was unsuccessful at first, then this encouraged consuming more gin. Modern medicine is replete with research concerning the adverse effects of binge drinking, and its effect upon unborn children.

- One other sad consequence of prolonged periods of binge drinking in the seventeenth century was the onset of sterility.

The references to 'Mother's ruin' are a sadly appropriate description of a period in gin's dark past. The modern world recognises this but consigns it to a very different world to the one we inhabit today.

Testing the 3Bs and D.I.S.T.I. L.

You've garnered an understanding of the D.I.S.T.I.L. process and now it's time to put theory to the test.

If you've followed the steps from Chapter One, you will have most of the equipment you need to proceed with Chapter Two. To recap, you need:

- A set of kitchen scales, to weigh botanicals, say up to 100 grams.[19]

- A set of measuring spoons.

- An A5-size notebook to record information in a diary format.

- A measuring cone, often used for measuring out small liquid quantities.

- A pipette for sampling purposes. A drinking straw, or a small polyethylene pipe connector are equally effective.

- A clean 500ml capacity water bottle. Repurposing a clean empty squeezable bottle is ideal.

As you can see from the list above, equipment needn't be expensive or specialist. Jar lids can act as glass covers to support organoleptic testing. Plastic tubing, such as a drinking straw, can act as a pipette for transferring gin samples to glasses. A conical cylinder allows you to measure water from the squeezable bottle for blending purposes. Inexpensive equipment for any gin making journey.

You will also need a copper still. Run a Google search for the search term 'copper alembic stills'. There are several models available, but the best starting kit is

---

21 This is key as the quantities to weigh will be fewer than 10 grams in most cases. A larger capacity weighing machine will make measuring small quantities very difficult.

one with a capacity of 1–2 litres. Be sure to include the following accessories to fit the still:

- Electric heating mantle
- Thermometer
- Hydrometer

DISTILLER'S PRO TIP

Before you buy your still, make sure that you have the following in place:

- Sufficient space available to use the still safely
- Safe access to a reliable source of electricity
- Safe access to a water supply with consistent flow
- Flexible hoses that can attach the still condenser to the water supply, and that allow water to discharge safely for collection and re-use

Once you make the purchasing decision, follow the instructions that describe how to use the still for the first time and regularly thereafter. Still maintenance is part and parcel for all successful operations, regardless of scale. The best strategy is to develop safe and consistent habits from the start.

Remember to record how you set everything up with pictures, recordings on your smartphone and notes in your trusty A5 notebook.

Most suppliers will sell this equipment in a complete kit for ease of purchase. Pre-used kits are often available at heavily discounted prices. Apply due diligence and ask lots of questions before committing to the purchase of pre-used equipment. A copper still is best, as demonstrated by 300 years of gin distillation.

DISTILLATION PROCESS

All science undergraduates learn about distilling processes. I was no different, and in fact took up the reins with distilling as part of high school chemistry. This was of course many years before I started making gin, and well before distilling became part and parcel of my undergraduate degree in chemistry. Chemistry graduates will attest to the fact that there are diverse types of chemistry, such as analytical chemistry, organic chemistry, and physical chemistry. Physical chemistry is particularly interesting, as it considers how chemical compounds, elements, or other complex compounds, interact with surfaces. Suffice to say, when you're first learning distillation as an undergraduate chemist, you're typically using glassware. Glass, to all intents and purposes, is inert and unreactive to most fluids. Glass provides visibility but not a lot else. Any reactivity that takes place within the glass container is solely between the molecules themselves. Even then, the materials require some affinity for one another, otherwise there would be no chemistry whatsoever.

Copper can conduct heat at about double the rate of aluminium and around ten times that of steel. This makes copper the best material to deal with water/ alcohol mixtures and heat, the cornerstones of any distilling operation. As an aside, scientific research suggests that copper is also highly antibacterial. Copper has antimicrobial properties[20] that can stop bacteria, viruses and algae dead in their tracks. Various copper compounds are used in industrial applications as catalysts; items that speed up reactions and reduce processing times. So not only is copper a good heat conductor – key for any distillation process – it presents opportunities for additional interactions, however minor, to take place during the distillation process.

Distilling gin – End to end

Let's put the process steps into action by deciding what kind of gin you would like to make. Based on the book content to this point you have an amazing array of assets at your disposal.

Let's recap what these are by reinforcing what you know from this book so far.

---

20 https://en.wikipedia.org/wiki/Antimicrobial_properties_of_copper

The five sample bases from the 3Bs will produce five different gin styles, albeit after a fixed period of steeping and some minor filtration steps.

By considering the gin in parts – like the musical parts in a three-piece band – you can select notes that interest you, and by extension, the botanicals that can deliver this.

The Advanced Botanical Lexicon shows you that using plain language will help identify and select several botanicals that can provide you with variations on the notes you need.

Objective reasoning provides you with an approach to assess the pros and cons for a series of options, and to make a considered choice by comparing each one.

There is no right or wrong answer; there is only the best answer for you to express your gin your way.

If you take a moment to reflect upon these key concepts, you can feel justifiably confident about stepping into the next stage of your gin making journey.

Decide

Here is the key question to answer in this step:

Based upon what I know and what I have, what botanicals would I need to create my own gin?

This is very much a planning exercise where you take creative ideas and concepts, write them down in plain language and then think through an approach. Here is a list of questions to consider as you mull through D.I.S.T.I.L.'s Decision step.

Start by reviewing your notes from the five bases, paying particular attention to Base II.

- What are the key notes and characteristics you would like your gin to have?

- Does a specific base – or your own variation – stand out as a starting point?

- Was there a base or several bases that were close to what you would like? If so, which botanicals do you think would improve the base?

- Which supporting botanicals would improve it for you?

- Which base botanicals would you reduce in quantity?

- Which base botanicals would you replace?

- Which botanicals would you add to the base?

Use plain English to describe the potential changes. The result of this planning process will be a series of experiments to consider during the Test stage of the D.I.S.T.I.L. process.

Investigate

Here is the key question to answer in this step:

Is there anyone out there who shares similar gin making ideas with me?

Once you have worked through the list of questions as a starting point, run an online search for gins that may have similar characteristics to your own. The botanical listings will be available in most cases, but without known quantities. A good place to start is with the gins you enjoy and admire. It is here where you can apply your judgement concerning Bases from the 3Bs. Reading gin reviews and garnering expert opinions is a good yet undervalued start. Note the key observations from these experts in your A5 notebook, noting who said what and when. The key descriptors that reviewers use is invaluable in your quest to find what will be a potential working guide for your gin. Look at a broad array of reviews – including different reviews for the same product – and maintain your relentless curiosity. When something takes your fancy it's time for the next step.

Sample

Here is the key question to answer in this step:

From my gin investigations which ones are worth sampling?

Pick up a sample of the gin or gins that appeal to you the most. Apply the skills you have learnt from 3Bs – Blending with water and assess the gins. Maintain that feeling of confidence – 'like a boss' – in your ability to prepare the samples for this step. Describe your experiences with each gin and make sure that you maintain good records for future reference as always. One other matter to consider at this stage is that sampling may start and end at your discretion. There is no set time or limit to the extent you may choose to sample the various gins you choose. Refer to any review material you may have concerning the gin; this will add richness to MI6-style investigations. But remember, amid all the energy and excitement this step can generate, do not lose sight of the objective. Sampling is the preparatory step you take in attempts to marry simple product descriptions of known gins (your samples) with the gin you would like to create. At the end of this process, your intent needs to be one where you can assess your experiences and apply what you've learnt. The learning process will help you confirm, dismiss, reassess or modify the characteristics you would like to experience in your gin. This leads to your first testing leap of faith.

Test

Here is the key question to answer in this step:

How do I put my ideas to the test?

You will recall from the D.I.S.T.I.L. process overview that this is the most demanding step in the D.I.S.T.I.L. process. You are about to find out why, as the following array experiments (in the Test and Improve steps) will attest.

3Bs meets D.I.S.T.I.L. head-on

This is where the real fun begins. You will need to do two things – which is in fact the same thing twice – but you will understand the method in the madness: 1) create a gin control by steeping the botanicals in vodka following the 3Bs process; 2) create a gin still charge by repeating the steps in 1) for use in the D.I.S.T.I.L. process.

Chances are you may already have a Base II gin available from Chapter One. This will act as the base control for comparison with X1. If not, you can always refer to the notes you've taken in your A5 notebook concerning your Base II observations as part of the 3Bs process.

For this exercise I've taken the known botanicals for Base II and made changes. Each change represents adjusting one botanical or botanical quantity in efforts to build the flavour profile that you would like your gin to possess.

Botanical base II, X1 and X2

Botanical	Base II	X1	X2
Juniper (grams)	**12.0**	12.0	12.0
Coriander (grams)	**3.0**	3.0	3.0
Lemon rind (grams)	**3.0**		
Lemon pieces	**3.0**	3.0	3.0
Orange strips	**3.0**	3.0	3.0
Liquorice Root sticks			1.0
Cassia (grams)		1.0	1.0
Fennel (grams)	**1.0**	1.0	1.0
Allspice (grams)	**1.0**	1.0	1.0
Cloves (grams)	**2.0**	2.0	2.0
Changes applied		No lemon	Add liquorice

Improve

Here is the key question to answer in this step:

How can I make my gin better than last time?

Let's see what we can do to improve the gin.

Here is a new list of experiments where the intent is to improve on Base II and some of the minor adjustments made so far.

Botanical bases II, X3, X4 and X5

Botanical	Base II	X3	X4	X5
Juniper (grams)	**12.0**	12.0	12.0	12.0
Coriander (grams)	**3.0**	3.0	3.0	3.0
Lemon rind (grams)	**3.0**			
Lemon pieces	**3.0**	1.5	1.5	1.5
Orange strips	**3.0**	3.0	3.0	3.0
Liquorice Root sticks		1.0	1.0	1.0
Cassia (grams)		1.0	1.0	1.0
Fennel (grams)	**1.0**	1.0	1.0	1.0
Allspice (grams)	**1.0**	1.0		
Cloves (grams)	**2.0**	2.0	2.0	
Changes applied		½ lemon	No allspice	No cloves

Note that these experiments use one important concept: build upon the base by changing one botanical or botanical quantity at a time. If you change more than one botanical, it will be unclear which one needs revision if you do not generate the result you need. We've kept juniper and coriander unchanged and noted the other changes at the bottom of the table.

Recall from Chapter One how the five mother sauces underwent minor changes to create new sauces that met a different need. The new sauce developments started off in a similar fashion to that described above:

take a known base (sauce), change one item (experiment) and review the result (new sauce).

Distilling run – X2

The following table illustrates an actual distillation run using Base II variant X2; add liquorice, ½ the lemon quantity. The still has a 6-litre capacity alembic handmade by Portuguese coppersmiths. The still charge is 1 litre of vodka with the botanical quantities adjusted upward by a factor of five. Heating mantle is set to five at the start. I recorded all of my observations on my smartphone, including some commentary and video for future reference.

Time, temperature and comments

Time	Temperature (Celsius)	Comments
18:26	25.0	Nothing to add
18:27	35.0	Heating mantle reduced from 5 to 3
18:28	65.0	Some lag before heat drops off
18:29	70.0	Some lag before heat drops off No leaks, cooling water flow OK
18:31	75.0	Some lag before heat drops off
18:48	77.0	Initial fraction, approx. 200 drips per minute

(Continued)

Time	Temperature (Celsius)	Comments
18:51	78.0	Start collecting distillate fraction
18:56	79.0	Taste test – OK (4 parts water, 1 part distillate)
19:00	80.0	Taste test – OK (4 parts water, 1 part distillate)
19:05	81.0	Taste test – OK (4 parts water, 1 part distillate)
19:10	82.0	Taste test – OK (4 parts water, 1 part distillate)
19:12	84.0	Flow rate starting to slow, aroma sharper
19:15	86.0	Aroma sharp, taste test poor Distillate collected still OK Stop collecting distillate Final temperature 90° Celsius

These performance details provided the basis to re-run the still with different experimental quantities for comparison and contrast; changing one botanical at a time.

The final distillate yield was around 350ml, at a strength of ~92% alcohol by volume. I then reduced 50ml of the distillate with 150ml of water and applied the Testing process for comparison with a standard Base II I had distilled earlier.

Including liquorice made a discernible positive difference, as did the reduction in lemon content.

PRO TIP

The distillation process generates significant heat. You must exercise caution at all times and observe safe practices. The need for diligence in this regard becomes more important at the end of a distillation run. Collect the distillate and keep it stored safely away from heat and open any flames. A clean, clear resealable glass jar or bottle labelled with the product details (date, time, name) is perfect.

Allow the pot still a reasonable time to cool down before carrying out the maintenance instructions that accompany the still. You will be left with an array of spent botanicals in hot liquid requiring disposal. For the green-thumbed gardeners amongst you, these materials are perfect for composting. For those with a culinary bent, you may be able to put the botanicals to use in other items such as marmalade, sauces or stock. One of the best examples of spent botanical repurposing is a delicious marmalade called Breakfast Negroni™ from Four Pillars. This is an industrial scale application that epitomises the 3Bs (botanicals, bases, blending) to a tee. Safely applying your sense of relentless curiosity can result in truly imaginative outcomes

Advanced botanical lexicon

Chapter One presented you with a series of core flavour descriptions that help gin makers to group botanicals into some semblance of order.

These are:

- Floral

- Fruity

- Spicy

- Woody

- Herbal

- Nutty

- Citrus

You may also recall from Chapter One how the five mother sauces were the basis for other products such as Mornay sauce or puttanesca.

This section will take a similar approach, expanding the current list into additional, more nuanced descriptions.

The value-add here though lies not so much in the descriptions themselves, but in deciding which botanical can best represent the description. In other words, if you can use plain language to describe what you want, then there is a direct connection to botanicals that may be useful in meeting this need. The caveat with this is as follows. Some of the botanicals may be unavailable, may be costly, in short supply, seasonal, or may not store well. Bear this in mind when considering the description guide.

THE BENEFITS OF PLAIN LANGUAGE

In the early 1990s, I was working on my first project in a new product development role with United Distillers Australia (now Diageo). The marketing brief concerned the combination of two iconic products from Bundaberg, a well-known region in rural Queensland. Each of these products were giants in their market and as such the opportunity to work in collaboration with some of Australia's finest producers was both rare and exciting. The Bundaberg Distilling company produces Australia's most popular rum products. Electra Breweries produce Australia's finest ginger beer. One of the unexpected takeaways from this project was the use of clear unambiguous language to describe exactly what was in the product: Dark & Stormy™. At the time, I didn't think too much of this, but over the years it has become clearer to me why language and clear expression are so important. If you cannot clearly describe the outcome that you seek, then it can be difficult for a team to help you achieve this. The labels describing Dark & Stormy clearly stated the use of Bundaberg Rum and Bundaberg Ginger beer.

Along with key stakeholders in each organisation
I oversaw the initial production runs take place in
two different manufacturing plants. Ten thousand
cases of Dark & Stormy were bottled at the Electra
Breweries' Bundaberg plant in May 1993. Ten
thousand cases of Dark & Stormy were canned at
the Huntingwood plant in Sydney in August of the
same year. Interestingly, in its first year all the stock
was slated for consumption in Queensland only.
A test market was set up in Newcastle, about two
hours' drive north of Sydney, which ultimately led
to producing this iconic product for markets outside
Queensland in the second year. And then when
Dark & Stormy started to hit its straps in 1994, the
sales teams invited people from any function in
the business to help deploy pop-up display stands
in as many Sydney-based bottle shops as possible.
The initiative kicked off at what is now the Sydney
Olympic Park precinct at Homebush and was dubbed
'The Bundy Blitz'. This was pivotal in cementing a
quintessentially Queensland product, in Australia's
most populous city. More than twenty-five years
later, people are still enjoying this iconic legacy.

Building out the descriptions

Let's consider each of the flavour descriptions above
in turn, expand upon these, and provide a suggested
botanical source. You will find that in all practicality,

some of these botanicals may not be available in your local region. This is where your sense of relentless curiosity will come to the fore. The gaps in the tables provide you with an opportunity to put your own local knowledge and research to work. It is remarkable how many hitherto unknown people are in the community with knowledge of local, state or national flora, who may be able to help find botanicals with comparable properties.

After all, tertiary institutions are bulging with botany students and experts, so these people may prove to be invaluable resources to supplement any online research you may choose to undertake.

Botanical assessments

How long will it take to choose botanicals? There will be a degree of trial and error in your efforts to build knowledge and apply what you've learnt. This could take anywhere from hours to days, depending upon where you are in the selection process. The best approach is to steep a native botanical, or some other botanical that you've not tried before, and assess what you get. It's simple to do, it's low cost, low risk, and easily controllable. And remember: the A5 notebook is your key to future success.

By collating your observations, it becomes a simple exercise to decide whether a botanical is worth keeping. If you decide that it is, well then leverage the third B – Blending – and blend it with one of the bases. A good shortcut to determining if a botanical would work, is to blend it with an existing gin. This is the simplest and fastest way to make an assessment. The acid test of course comes down to when you start using that botanical in the base, and start distilling the products you intend to work through for your gin. As you'll know from Steps 4 and 5 in the D.I.S.T.I.L. process, there is a significant amount of valuable work involved, but the 'fast and furious', low risk, low cost approach is to start steeping and then apply your knowledge as you see fit.

Botanical quality

Ensuring high quality consistent supply at a reasonable cost is a challenge for gin makers.

This is why due consideration to readily available botanicals, which are in plentiful supply, and are of consistent quality is so important. This approach reduces risk. If you've got a consistent supply, it's always good value to have more than one supplier. If for example you have a European supplier and a southern hemisphere supplier, it means that there may be some variations between the botanicals that you're interested in. What you can do is blend each supplier's botanicals together to create a level of consistency between the two groups. Potentially, this means that you can have botanicals available all year round. It's one way to iron out some perceived quality inconsistencies between botanicals.

Additional botanicals

This table provides a straightforward guide to match an intended description to a specific botanical. The botanical choice will require tempering of course with matters such as availability, cost, perishability and so forth. But as an initial guide, there are several botanicals here that can make an invaluable contribution to your gin making efforts. This is merely a sample or tip of the botanical iceberg but does serve to illustrate the range of gins that are possible with fewer than forty botanicals to work with. For example, if you're after a fleshy fruit characteristic for your gin, then any one or several of grapes, mangoes or peaches will do the trick.

Guide to botanicals

Grouping	Characteristic	Botanical
Citrus Botanicals	Acid	Grapefruit
Citrus Botanicals	Acid	Lemon
Citrus Botanicals	Acid	Lime
Citrus Botanicals	Sweet	Navel oranges
Citrus Botanicals	Sweet	Tangelos
Floral Botanicals	Aromatic	Elderflower

(Continued)

Grouping	Characteristic	Botanical
Floral Botanicals	Fresh	Lavender
Floral Botanicals	Perfumed	Roses
Floral Botanicals	Perfumed	Violets
Fruit Botanicals	Fruity	Apples
Fruit Botanicals	Fleshy	Apricots
Fruit Botanicals	Red	Cherries
Fruit Botanicals	Fruity	Cucumbers
Fruit Botanicals	Fruity	Grapes
Fruit Botanicals	Fleshy	Mangoes
Fruit Botanicals	Fleshy	Peaches
Herbal Botanicals	Tasty	Fennel
Herbal Botanicals	Fresh	Mint
Herbal Botanicals	Fragrant	Rosemary
Herbal Botanicals	Fragrant	Sage
Herbal Botanicals	Fragrant	Thyme
Nutty Botanicals	Fragrant	Almonds
Nutty Botanicals	Woody	Chestnuts
Nutty Botanicals	Fragrant	Hazelnuts
Nutty Botanicals	Fragrant	Macadamias
Nutty Botanicals	Woody	Walnuts
Spicy Botanicals	Musky	Coriander
Spicy Botanicals	Fiery	Cubeb

(Continued)

Grouping	Characteristic	Botanical
Spicy Botanicals	Musky	Ginger
Spicy Botanicals	Fiery	Grains of paradise
Woody Botanicals	Dirty	Angelica root
Woody Botanicals	Warm	Cassia
Woody Botanicals	Warm	Orris

The following table is the corollary of the one above. In this case if you think of a botanical, this will give you an idea of what type of finish the botanical will bring to your finished gin product.

For example, if you're curious about using hazelnuts, this table suggests that including them will give you a fragrant nutty characteristic to your gin.

Botanical characteristics and groupings

Botanical	Characteristic	Grouping
Almonds	Fragrant	Nutty Botanicals
Angelica root	Dirty	Woody Botanicals
Apples	Fruity	Fruit Botanicals
Apricots	Fleshy	Fruit Botanicals
Cassia	Warm	Woody Botanicals
Cherries	Red	Fruit Botanicals
Chestnuts	Woody	Nutty Botanicals

(Continued)

Botanical	Characteristic	Grouping
Coriander	Musky	Spicy Botanicals
Cubeb	Fiery	Spicy Botanicals
Cucumbers	Fruity	Fruit Botanicals
Elderflower	Aromatic	Floral Botanicals
Fennel	Tasty	Herbal Botanicals
Ginger	Musky	Spicy Botanicals
Grains of paradise	Fiery	Spicy Botanicals
Grapefruit	Acid	Citrus Botanicals
Grapes	Fruity	Fruit Botanicals
Hazelnuts	Fragrant	Nutty Botanicals
Lavender	Fresh	Floral Botanicals
Lemon	Acid	Citrus Botanicals
Lime	Acid	Citrus Botanicals
Macadamias	Fragrant	Nutty Botanicals
Mangoes	Fleshy	Fruit Botanicals
Mint	Fresh	Herbal Botanicals
Navel oranges	Sweet	Citrus Botanicals
Orris root	Warm	Woody Botanicals
Peaches	Fleshy	Fruit Botanicals
Rosemary	Fragrant	Herbal Botanicals
Roses	Perfumed	Floral Botanicals

(Continued)

Botanical	Characteristic	Grouping
Sage	Fragrant	Herbal Botanicals
Tangelos	Sweet	Citrus Botanicals
Thyme	Fragrant	Herbal Botanicals
Violets	Perfumed	Floral Botanicals
Walnuts	Woody	Nutty Botanicals

Whenever you consider putting your own gin components together or developing a variation upon a gin product, the best place to start is by describing the characteristics you would like in your gin. Use plain language when doing so, because if the problem is simple to describe, then it becomes easier to solve. Simplicity in language is key. Be clear about your intent. Have clarity about what this means about the upfront taste, the palate, the finish, and the emotions that this evokes.

After some thought you may consider a more fragrant botanical. Examples could be honey myrtle, edelweiss or honeysuckle; kaffir lime is a worthwhile consideration as well.

The list of standard flavour characteristics to consider are simple.

Do you want to have a long peppery finish or one with a sweet note? For example, if you consider spicy botanicals, these may be best described as peppery, fiery or curried. A peppery spicy finish suggests using peppercorns, cubeb, or grains of paradise, the classic botanical used in Bombay Sapphire™ gin. Spiciness also lends itself to options such as star anise, curry leaf or green cardamom, another classic botanical that many distillers use in their gins.

Other spices include mountain horopito, cayenne, black pepper, white pepper or horseradish. Wasabi, popular as an addition when consuming sushi, is a cornerstone to simple Japanese cuisine that can hold its own as a gin botanical.

When considering other types of spice, sweet spices such as ginger, ginseng, or the classic coriander seed are worthy candidates. Coriander seed can complement ginger and ginseng, in the same way that cardamom is used as a complement to juniper berries. They're used in the culinary arts for several reasons. They have stood the test of time in a vast array of dishes because they produce great fragrances, aromas, and taste sensations. Moreover, they're durable, robust, and can withstand heat.

Other botanicals with popularity in the culinary arts include cumin, caraway seeds, or fennel seeds; curry leaf, green cardamom, star anise, cloves, all spice, cubeb, chilli; the range of botanicals available for use is breath-taking. Rooty botanicals such as angelica and orris are hands down the most popular and enduring.

Options such as gentian root can more than hold their own in this lofty company as well.

Nuts provide a welter of possibilities as well. Almonds are a classic botanical but the likes of hazelnuts, brazil nuts, pistachios, macadamias, pecans, nutmeg, and wattle seeds can hold their own in any still charge; the sky's the limit.

Perhaps you would like some more subtleties to come through: initially sweet, then easing down to something that's a bit spicier or a bit warmer?

You can also suppress or subdue spicy botanicals against something clean and fruity such as cucumber or apples. This produces a distinct set of notes which are wonderful to explore.

Cassia and cinnamon are warming botanicals. They may even connect you to fond memories in childhood, with biscuits or other sweet treats.

Let's think about descriptions for citrus botanicals: fleshy, juicy, zesty or sour.

Other classics are whole lemons, sliced lemons or lemon peel. Consider all peels: orange peel, lime peel, grapefruit peel. Citrus peel additions are readily available and bring a broad range of flavours to gin.

You may like to consider berries. Rhubarb – the queen of fruits – is a wonderful plant used predominantly in dessert cooking. Rhubarb matches particularly well with apple, to make rhubarb and apple crumble. These tried and trusted flavours from the culinary arts elicit a sense of belonging and delight. This is even more pronounced if you consumed them in great quantities in childhood. A fantastic dessert after a Sunday roast meal, and an excellent consideration for gin.

Blackberries grow wild, and their flavour is remarkable. Likewise, cherries are an interesting fruit, that will remind many people of Christmas. Strawberries are available in many different varieties. Kiwi fruit – also known as Chinese gooseberries or kiwis – are a little bit harder to find but have an inherent fleshiness that is worth exploring.

Quinces are amazing. They are great in jam, as they tolerate heat well, making them a tremendous addition to any still charge. The flavours are fantastic. The balance is there albeit a little jammy for some palates. Don't let this stop you from experimenting with this remarkable old-fashioned fruit; it does require a lot of preparation to get the best out of your quinces, however. Those who have made quince jam are likely to know this because of the amount of pectin that needs breaking down; however, this characteristic lends itself well to gin making. It's robust. It can stand the heat, harsh treatment and it's a tremendous botanical if you can get your hands on it.

Berries may be tangy, jammy, plump, sweet or candied. And then are other fruit options such as melon, rock melon, apple, sweet navel orange, pineapple, mango, nectarines, apricots, tangerines, pomelos – all outstanding botanicals with loads of potential.

Peaches are a delicate botanical to consider. I have vivid childhood memories of eating peaches, grown in the backyard of my home in 1970s Auckland. Biting into the fleshy skin, juice that would drip down your chin as you savour every bite, to the point where you bit the stone in the middle. Sometimes the basis for a botanical selection may be about evoking emotions in simple ways. Expressing this range of emotions can help bring your gin making efforts to life and create their own positive energy.

There is always a place for sweet botanicals in any gin. Vanilla and liquorice root are classic botanicals used by many gin makers over the years. Mint, geraniums, jasmine, lavender and roses have a place in the sweet botanical lexicon as well.

Pears are an underrated fleshy fruit, with a sense of subtlety about them. A variation on a pear is the nashi. In New Zealand, there are feijoas, also referred to as a pineapple guava in Australia. This fruit brings a jammy characteristic to gin which is difficult to replicate in any other way.

These thoughts can provide ways for you to creatively express how you would like your gin to taste.

Consider what's readily available in your area, from your supermarket or from your grower. Consider which part of the flavour spectrum this resides in. What this then means is that you can do a bit of mix and match with your botanical selections.

The whole key is to start with simple terms and spend time thinking about the outcomes you would like to see. Making a few inquiries concerning the botanicals will provide you with an excellent start.

Consider this example of how a simple idea has gone on to great things

CHASE DISTILLERY

The Chase Distillery use apples as the basis for creating an outstanding gin. Chase grow their apples on their farm, they make cider as the base and use that as the key to a process of multiple distillations. Chase produces a gin which is rich in flavour. It's an expression of their heritage, their connection with the land and the importance of knowing the grower and bringing the gin from farm to bottle. It's this kind of emotive connection that a gin maker can bring to life and express through their craft.

In more recent times manuka honey has gained popularity, particularly in New Zealand, where the manuka tree grows prolifically, providing bees with the resources they need to produce honey.

Another botanical gaining popularity is yuzu, both as an addition to gin and for use in tonic water. East Imperial™ produce a Yuzu tonic water product which is tremendous with certain gins. It complements sweeter gins well but has lots of potential as a still charge botanical.

If we consider the term 'floral', this would include botanicals as diverse as hibiscus, chamomile or elder-flower; this last one is a popular choice in some of Britain's finest gins. The hidden charm of floral botanicals lies in their aroma; lavender is a case in point. It makes sense to consider chamomile as a botanical, as people drink chamomile tea. It's calming, aromatic and yet uplifting when harmonising with other botanicals.

Grassy botanicals include gems such as leafy lemon verbena or lemon myrtle, very popular in Australia.

Herbal botanicals have a range of characteristics too. A savoury herb, for example, may accompany an evening meal, and have the potential to be in a finished gin. Oregano, marjoram or rosemary are examples of everyday botanicals that people consume on a regular basis. These can be particularly useful adjuncts to what you want to put together for your gin.

A right-field excursion would be to consider sarsaparilla – the basis of root beer – barley or Madagascan vanilla as used in Hernö Gin™ from Sweden.[21]

Revising how the magic ratios break down will provide you with starting point quantities, and these provide you with a framework. Expanding on this concept will reveal diverse ways that can allow you to express the way you want your gin to be.

Botanical magic – Ink's triumph for Art and Science

There is a remarkable botanical which holds the key to one of the most scientifically spectacular gins that you can come across: the gin called Ink.[22] The key to its success lies with carefully treating the butterfly-pea flower (*Clitoria ternatea*) and managing pH concentrations in the finished product.

The most remarkable aspect of this beautiful blue-coloured gin reveals itself with the addition of tonic. The colour changes from blue to a wonderful pink. It's a triumph of science, nature, perseverance and some sharp chemistry.

---

21 https://hernogin.com
22 https://inkgin.com

Mixer magic – a triumph for gin and tonic

Beer, wine, cola, rum, gin, bourbon tea, coffee and flavoured milk are common examples that describe different categories of beverage. Few of the beverages in their respective categories possess the same taste or flavour characteristics, as manufacturers provide their own production processes and methods in each case. No two beers, or flavoured milk products taste exactly the same.

Tonic, like any beverage, is a many splendoured thing. There are many tonic formulations but, by and large, they all have one taste component in common. The bitter taste that sets tonic apart comes from quinine. The source of quinine in most cases is from a plant found in the Congo, called the cinchona, also known colloquially as the fever tree. The Fever Tree™ name is synonymous with an outstanding brand of tonic, but also provides an example writ large. Fever Tree have no fewer than four outstanding tonics which gin enthusiasts can select. The folks at Fever Tree recognised that no two gins are alike, so it made sense to create tonic waters with this notion top of mind. This means that Fever Tree – and other tonic producers such as East Imperial – provide a means for all gin enthusiasts to find the ideal match for their favourite gin.

For those with a scientific bent, there is a simple way to distinguish differing quality between tonics that you may consider.

The quinine molecule is chemically interesting, as it has a double aromatic ring. An aromatic ring in this context is a structural chemistry term, used to describe a flat ring of atoms that is particularly stable. This term is not one related to the sense of smell. The fact that quinine has two of these rings – depicted as hexagons at the base of the molecule – means that it will react to black light (ultraviolet light). The amount of glow is directly proportional to the amount of quinine used in the tonic water.

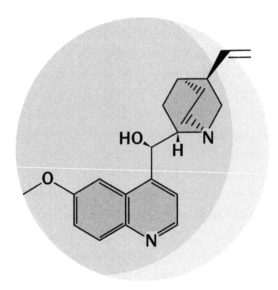

The molecular structure of quinine

So, if you'd like to dazzle your friends with science, put a bottle of tonic water, soda water and lemonade next to each without labels. Ask your friends to pick the bottle with the tonic water in it. Sheer guess work means they will have a one in three chance of being correct. Once they've made their choice, dim the lights and break out the black light and point it at the bottles.

Try repeating the exercise with tonic water made by different manufacturers and you will see the stark differences between each product.

Think of it as a nostalgic trip to the decadent eighties when big hair, shoulder pads, thin leather ties and frequenting night clubs was *de rigeur*. For those who weren't there, you don't know what you missed. And for those of you that were there, you probably wish you had.

What distinguishes high quality gin from poor quality gin?

The simplest way is to try it! If the gin is to your taste and is consistent with your expectations from high quality gin, then you're more than half way there. You could also consider the manufacturing process. Distillation processes produce a more complete and robust product, whose characteristics are consistent with people's expectations for a product called gin. Gins that do not use distillation techniques deny the gin makers the opportunity for complex flavour development and integration between the botanicals. Forged under direct controlled energy and high temperatures, the botanicals undergo interactions that reflect the complexities of flavour development, and purification. Another way is by appearance, but even that's becoming a bit more subjective, with more and more barrel-aged gins making their mark. These will often have sediment collecting at the bottom of the gin bottle. Moreover, the gin will no longer be clear and transparent, and it may have a slight tinge of yellow, which in the good old days was a bit of a tell-tale sign that maybe the gin was neither distilled nor of good quality. In today's modern rendition of the gin legacy it could be regarded as a signature mark for a manufacturing process. Dirty June Barrel Reserve Gin™ [23] being a case in point.

Ultimately quality gin, food or music share a lot of common ground. Something that's been around for a long time appeals to different tastes for different people and at different times. Quality gin comprises a balance between characteristics that stand out. Among these are clarity of flavour, the cleanness, the complexities that you get when you taste it, and the fact that you can actually mix it with things of your choice that you enjoy. Ultimately, it can be somewhat subjective. What may be your favourite may in fact be an acquired taste to someone else. This makes exploration and sharing ideas all the more interesting and exciting for people to pursue.

---

23 https://bonespirits.com/quick-facts

Summary

Simplicity is key.

Describe everything in plain language, and with the overall taste journey front of mind.

- The aroma – what aroma characteristics are you after?

- The first taste – what first impression do you intend to make?

- The palate – how do you want it to feel when you take a sip of it? Do you want it to be sweet?

- The finish – Do you want it to be smooth? Do you want it to be spicy? Do you want it to complement your favourite tonic?

Nutty, sweet, herbal, grassy, floral, berries, fruity, citrusy, spicy; simple terms that are easy to understand. These plain language descriptors will help you choose a botanical from the many options available.

Consider this general thought concerning potential botanicals. If you can make tea with a botanical it's worth investigating. This means that it can handle the heat, the pressure, turbulence and reflux that takes place inside a still; proof positive of its value as a wonderful botanical; flavours undergo their release and add to the lexicon that you're producing. This serves to add more value to any planned outcomes you have in mind as a gin maker.

The range of different botanical options and varieties is exciting in so many ways. The key though is to temper the approach with restraint with this simple concept; always remember that less is more.

The last word on botanical numbers – Less is more

Let's bring things back again. After the energy and excitement that endless botanical possibilities can provide, the best place to start is with one that is consistent with the 'less is more' mantra.

Gins do not need to be nutty, sweet, rooty, spicy and herbal, grassy, floral or fruity all at once.

Carefully consider and select the flavour groups and botanicals you want and then pick the style that you like. Use some of the classic descriptions from the giants of the gin making trade as a basis for working out what you would like to see in your gin.

Consider no more than ten botanicals covering three to four flavour groups.

This apparent constraint appears limiting until you consider the five bases from the 3Bs in Chapter One. By selecting more than ten botanicals, there is a risk that some flavour profiles you seek will be over-run. This hinders the ability of the full botanical line-up to fully develop during the reflux process and express themselves. Think of a musical instrument in a three-piece band that dominates their intended sound.

These are characteristics that need to be near and dear to you. Take the framework and express yourself as a musician or chef would do. No two songs sound the same, no two dishes deliver the same experience, even if some would suggest otherwise. A song and a dish are expressions of the artist, and the outcome they want to share with the audience. Treat your gin making the same way. Take the passion that you have for the botanicals, the passion that you have for gin making, pull all of that together and express the gin your way.

In so doing, you will develop a level of authenticity that is truly yours. You'll create your own legacy, and not an under-done impression of something else. The gin will be an extension of who you are. There will be a degree of heritage around it, so guard it. Guardianship is important so be true to yourself when you take on the gin making journey.

HOW MANY BOTANICALS DOES A LONDON DRY GIN USE?

Although there is no hard and fast rule concerning botanical numbers, most London Dry Gins will have between five and twelve botanicals most of the time.

There other gins that may use greater or fewer botanicals in their creation.

Monkey 47 is one of the most complex examples of a gin with a lot of botanicals in it. This still means though that botanical choices, quantities and numbers come down to personal taste and bringing your style to the gin making art. My philosophy has always been that less is more. I've not been terribly keen on overlaying botanical listings as far as gins are concerned, the reason being that there are only so many combinations that you can put together before a botanical's value in the gin starts to diminish and becomes almost non-existent.

There are some gins that have more, but again it's a matter of taste. If you put on your musical hat again, groups like Cream and Green Day have three members, the Beatles had four members, the Dave Clark Five had... well... five people. Even orchestras, with their vast array of people, have few groups of instruments in play. Strings, woodwind, percussion, brass are the cornerstones of an orchestra, but with variations within those groupings. For example, the wind instruments may comprise flutes, oboes, clarinets and bassoons. Think lemon peel, dried peel, peel zests of different flavours and the analogies are easy to see.

CHAPTER THREE

Gin As A Global Phenomenon

This chapter will describe how access to modernised versions of nineteenth century technology gave rise to the massive production of globally significant gin brands. These brands set the tone for twentieth century consumers. You will learn how another technological step-change toward the latter part of the twentieth century helped to catalyse the small batch distilling movement to prominence in the twenty-first century.

One exciting by-product of the small batch distilling movement is the large array of botanicals the next generation are putting to use. Chapter Two explored a selection of these botanicals as an extension to the 3Bs work touched upon in Chapter One.

Let's begin this third chapter with a trip through history, to set the scene for what was to become a global phenomenon that was centuries in the making.

What is gin's origin?

There are some references – albeit rather tenuous – that doctors used an alcohol and juniper concoction to cure kidney and bladder complaints in 1650s Europe. The most renowned of these people was a Dutch physician named Franciscus Sylvius de Bouve (1614–1672). That said, there is no firm evidence to support any claim that gin's origins are linked to him. The next piece of history will also cast doubts to this claim.

In 1618 – when Sylvius was four years of age – British and Dutch soldiers fought side by side during periods of the Thirty Years war (1618–1648).[24] This conflict was waged by European protestants in response to the appointment of the staunchly Roman Catholic ruler Ferdinand II as Holy Roman Emperor, King of Bohemia, and King of Hungary. The soldiers consumed a Dutch drink called jenever. Jenever was made from distilling malt wine, and then tempering its flavour with an array of botanicals, including juniper. Soldiers would typically drink this concoction before going into battle. Consuming jenever appears to be

---

24 https://history.com/topics/thirty-years-war

the origin of the term Dutch Courage.[25] Interestingly, the French word for juniper is *genièvre*. By contracting this word and the word genever we end up with the word gin. This would make complete sense to our Australian readers, who have turned the contraction of lengthy – and even not so lengthy – words into a linguistic artform.

History also tells us that gin first came to Britain when the Dutch monarch William of Orange[26] set foot in Devon to rule Britain in 1688. By taking the throne from his father-in-law King James II for both himself and his wife Mary II, he became William III of England, and was also affectionately known as King Billy of Scotland and Ireland.

This gives gin an undisputed connection with royalty and privilege, but in the years to come it would be the drink of choice for all.

One of the first decrees or decisions William took as King was to give gin making an unfettered run to commercialisation. Those keen to make gin paid an administration fee to customs and after ten days they were in business. There was an excess of grain available at the time, deemed unfit for human consumption. This provided a valuable and inexpensive raw material for gin production.

---

25 https://gintime.com/features/
dutch-courage-a-short-history-of-dutch-jenever
26 https://en.wikipedia.org/wiki/William_III_of_England

The British Mutiny Act of 1720 further encouraged gin production. Gin makers were exempt from billeting soldiers. This led to innkeepers making gin, which was great for gin entrepreneurs at the time. The opportunity for innkeepers to avoid having to house unwanted guests proved to be a great catalyst for gin production.

Consider this. London's population was around 600,000 people at this time. Access to gin and its legal consumption were easy to carry out. In some ways, the conditions were perfect for the first drug epidemic, one that was forged and fuelled by the poor and disadvantaged.

Gin was inexpensive to make, had little or no competition in the marketplace and so a popular and profitable business began to thrive.

DOES GIN HAVE THERAPEUTIC QUALITIES?

Interestingly, gin has a history of use 'for medicinal purposes'. For example, in the late thirteenth century, a Dutch publication described juniper-based health-related tonics.

The Royal Navy mixed gin with lime cordial to stop scurvy, and angostura settled the stomach at sea. In life, there is the age-old adage that refuses to go away; everything in moderation.

There was also a firmly held belief in mid to late seventeenth century Europe that juniper berries had positive medicinal impacts. History suggests that a Dutch scientist, Franciscus Sylvius de Bouve, had an interest in all manner of tinctures, one of which was a juniper base. His interest helped to reinforce the view that juniper berries did have some form of medicinal benefit for those who consumed them as part of a mixture of alcohol.

The more modern equivalent of this may be drawn from the malaria prevention steps that nineteenth century British soldiers took during postings to India via gin and tonic.[27]

Whether their view is maintained in today's modern society is a moot point, but the best position to take is one that maintains that anything in moderation will have some form of benefit to it. Issues may arise however when over-use becomes abuse and dependency if left unattended.

Finally, the most recent assertion concerning gin's health benefits came to light in Sarah Young's June 2017 article entitled 'Drinking Gin and Tonics could soothe hay fever symptoms, study finds'.[28]

The article compares histamine levels with various alcoholic beverages. Research reveals that there are lower amounts of histamine in white spirits –

27 https://wearethemighty.com/history/gin-tonic-military-origins
28 https://independent.co.uk/life-style/hayfever-gin-tonics-vodka-spirits-sooth-symptoms-allergies-histamines-sulphates-asthma-uk-study-a7800216.html

including gin – than in other alcoholic beverages. According to Asthma UK, this means that consuming white spirits is the best option to pursue if you are a hay fever sufferer. This advice may need tempering insofar as consuming gin is not a 'magic bullet' cure-all for the symptoms hay fever sufferers experience.

Definitions – What makes gin 'gin'?

Let's fast forward to today and consider how different jurisdictions legally define and describe gin.

To refer to an alcoholic drink as 'Gin' it must take on the taste characteristics that are consistent with juniper berries. Different countries around the world express this requirement in slightly different ways. In the United States, gin is defined as:

'... an alcoholic beverage of no less than 40% ABV (80 proof) that possesses the characteristic flavour of juniper berries. Gin produced only through distillation or redistillation of aromatics with an alcoholic wash can be further distinguished and marketed as "distilled gin".'[29]

---

29 Definitions ('Standards of Identity') for Distilled Spirits, Title 27 of the U.S. Code of Federal Regulations, Chapter 1, Part 5, Section 5.22(c) Class 3

The Canadian Food and Drug Regulation recognises gin with three different definitions (Genever, Gin, London or Dry gin) that loosely approximate the US definitions. Whereas a more detailed regulation is provided for Holland gin or genever, no distinction is made between compounded gin and distilled gin. Either compounded or distilled gin can be labelled as Dry Gin or London Dry Gin if it does not contain any sweetening agents.[30]

IS GIN A DEPRESSANT OR STIMULANT?

Gin and most other alcoholic products act as depressants. Unfortunately, it does deaden your senses. That's the way alcohol operates. However, having said that, it does it in a cycle. Quite often, and this could be purely a function of the environment or the company that you're with, alcohol can give you a bit of a high to start with. In particular, if there are lots of people engaged, and there's a happy vibe where you are.

Ultimately however, over the longer period of time alcohol will begin to subdue the excitement or exhilaration that may associate with your first few sips. Gin follows a similar pattern, insofar as it's uplifting to start with, but then the effects of that uplift will drop off over a period of time.

---

30 'Food and Drug Regulations (C.R.C., c. 870)'. Justice Laws Website – Canada, Government of Canada.

In February 2008, the European Union passed a new gin definition into law, as part of the EU Spirit drink regulations, as follows.

All gins must be:[31]

1. Made with suitable ethyl alcohol flavoured with juniper berries (*Juniperus communis*) and other flavourings.

2. The ethyl alcohol used must be distilled to the minimum standards stated in the EU Spirit Drink Regulations.

3. The predominant flavour must be juniper.

4. Water may be added to reduce the strength, but the gin must have a minimum retail strength of 37.5% ac/vol.

5. Further ethyl alcohol of the same composition used in the distillation may be added after distillation.

Giants of distilled gin

The most enjoyable aspect about gin is its creative range. Every gin is unique. Any gin worthy of the name will always feature the piney flavour that comes from juniper. After all, that is the drink's cornerstone,

---

31 https://legislation.gov.uk/uksi/2008/3206/pdfs/
uksi_20083206_en.pdf

its key to existence. Here is a short timeline illustrating how enduring some brands are, despite relatively humble and difficult beginnings.

Greenalls Gin™ – 1761[32]

Bombay Sapphire – est. 1761, since 1987[33]

Gordon's Gin – 1769[34]

Plymouth Gin – 1793[35]

Tanqueray Gin™ – 1830[36]

Beefeater Gin™ – 1876[37]

Hendrick's Gin™ – est. 1886[38], since 1999

You will soon see that no two gins have identical botanical listings, and yet they remain as popular as ever among their followers. In some cases, this support spans hundreds of years and is arguably as strong and passionate today as it ever was.

The array of flavours is the fuel that keeps gin vibrant and relevant. Gin's followers keep coming back for

32 https://greenallsgin.com/greenalls-story
33 https://bombaysapphire.com
34 www.gordonsgin.com/en-row
35 http://plymouthgin.com
36 www.tanqueray.com
37 https://beefeatergin.com/en-EN/our-history
38 https://hendricksgin.com

more as ever-increasing numbers of creative people make their contributions to the gin legacy.

Twenty-first-century gin styles that suppress or subdue the juniper flavour are becoming more and more popular among a new generation of gin enthusiasts. In the spirit of London Dry Gin distinguishing itself from its Dutch connections with genever, these contemporary 'new kids on the block' are now commanding their own description, their own sound if you will, that sets them apart:

- New Western gin[39]

- International or New World gin[40]

- Contemporary gin,[41] whose momentum is linked to the small batch and craft distilling movement where juniper shares parity with other botanicals in the line-up

This has proven to be a godsend for brands such as Four Pillars, Hendrick's, Aviation™, Botanist™ and Poor Toms Sydney Dry Gin. A new wave of consumers has made themselves known, loudly and proudly, in the same age-old tradition that has punctuated gin's heritage for over 300 years.

---

39 https://theginisin.com/articles/
    what-is-new-american-or-new-western-gin
40 https://theginisin.com/articles/
    what-is-new-american-or-new-western-gin
41 https://theginisin.com/articles/
    what-is-new-american-or-new-western-gin/

Here are some outstanding gins and their respective lists of botanicals. You will note that these brands have variations on a common base. It's the supporting botanicals in the listing and the differences in production approach that set each of these and any other gin in the world apart from the others.

Very few gins are made the same way with the same botanicals listing despite sharing the same key bases as their respective starting point; recall the Green Day and Cream musical analogy.

This short selection of the world's finest is a demonstrative case in point.

The step-changes in technology that drove these brands into the global powerhouse that endure today are simple; larger numbers of bigger stills, and improved distribution links that took Britain's finest gin brands to the world.

Let's begin.

Tanqueray[42]

Since the 1870s. This is a single shot gin made in a pot still, the brainchild of Charles Tanqueray.

Nose: Fresh and smooth, with juniper and citrus

---

42 https://thespruceeats.com

Palate: Balanced and dry, with juniper, coriander and liquorice

Finish: Long and full, with juniper and a hint of pepper/spice

- Juniper
- Coriander
- Angelica root
- Liquorice

Gordon's Gin[43]

Since 1769, by Alexander Gordon.

Nose: Fresh with juniper and citrus

Palate: Dry and fresh, with juniper and citrus

Finish: Short and light, with juniper and citrus

- Juniper
- Coriander
- Angelica root
- Liquorice
- Orris root

---

43 https://theginguide.com/gordons-gin-review-and-tasting-notes. html

- Ginger
- Nutmeg
- Cassia oil
- Orange peel
- Lemon peel

Bombay Sapphire[44]

Since 1987, based on a recipe from 1761.

Nose: Sweet and aromatic, with citrus and juniper

Palate: Initially light, followed by spices and earthy notes

Finish: Sweet and lingering, with juniper and peppery spices

- Juniper
- Coriander
- Angelica root
- Liquorice
- Orris root
- Cubeb berries

---

44 https://theginguide.com/bombay-sapphire-gin-review-and-tasting-notes.html

- Lemon peel
- Almond
- Grains of paradise
- Cassia bark

Hendrick's[45]

Since 1999, the brainchild of Lesley Gracie, a fine distiller from Scotland whose passion for quality and excellence epitomises heritage, guardianship and legacy.

Nose: Fresh and floral, with sweet lime and light spices

Palate: Smooth, with rose and sweet citrus

Finish: Long and floral, with rose

- Juniper
- Coriander
- Angelica root
- Orris root
- Cubeb berry
- Lemon

---

45 https://theginguide.com/Hendricks-gin-review-and-tasting-notes.html

- Caraway

- Chamomile

- Elderflower

- Orange peel

- Yarrow

Marrying two gin distillation charges and infusing this with rose petals and cucumber sets this gin apart. The Hendrick's team have taken the use of rose petals to a new level of sophistication. Pairing this with cucumber merely reinforces its reputation as a gin without peer.

Poor Toms Gin in Marrickville, NSW, marries two gin distillation charges in a similar fashion – albeit with a differing array of botanicals – to reflect quintessentially Australian origins.

Beefeater

Since the 1870s,[46] founded by James Burrough with first production taking place in 1876 at the Chelsea Distillery he bought for £400 in 1863.[47]

Nose: Clean and earthy, with juniper and citrus

---

46 https://theginguide.com/beefeater-gin-review-and-tasting-notes.html
47 https://beefeatergin.com/our-history

Palate: Smooth and clean, with orange and coriander

Finish: Sweet and lingering, with orange and coriander

- Juniper
- Coriander
- Liquorice
- Almond
- Orris root
- Orange peel
- Lemon peel

Visual assessment tools

The Gin Pentagon[48]

In January of 2015, Poor Toms Gin in Sydney, Australia, hosted a kick off meeting to launch their foray into the burgeoning craft gin market. As part of the kick off, the co-founders held an event for immediate family and friends, most of whom knew little about gin, let alone the gin making process.

As an ice-breaker to the event, a small team comprising myself and the co-founders facilitated a fun workshop where people received instructions concerning

---

48 https://theginisin.com/our-philosophy/a-new-way-to-review-gin

the best way to sample and test an array of gins that were available for the event. We provided samples of the botanicals they would expect to encounter and used simple descriptions to cater for the broad range of experience the audience brought with them.

The gin pentagon – the brainchild and generous gift[49] from Aaron Knoll of the GIN is IN – provides a way for people to gauge flavour intensity from 1 to 3 (low to high intensity) concerning five specific characteristics. If a participant was unable to discern one of the five they merely scored this a zero and dropped it from the assessment.

- Juniper characteristics
- Citrus/fruity characteristics
- Spicy/hot characteristics
- Alcoholic characteristics
- Floral characteristics

Each gin was reduced in strength by half and allowed to stand for 10 minutes before serving to each participant. The process generated a lot of audience interest and was a fantastic way for people to meet up, converse and get to know one another a little better.

---

49 https://theginisin.com/news/
    why-im-releasing-my-flavor-diagram-for-you-to-use

There were some interesting insights that came about too. The power of the crowd cannot be understated when it comes to gauging concepts that are hard to measure. We found that the younger generation of testers were particularly sensitive to high alcohol characters, preferring gins that were sweeter on the palate. Several of our younger folks created pentagons that rated the alcoholic characteristic as 3.

The young at heart, however, were not impressed by the sweeter gins, preferring the more robust offerings on show. The team reviewed this feedback and used it as the basis for objective reasoning concerning the gin we wanted to create. Two weeks after this event, the race to create a world class gin for Poor Toms was underway. Eight weeks later we got there, on the Thursday before Easter 2015.

Note too that the Gin Pentagon was customised to the audience. The terms and concepts were easy to understand; providing physical examples of the botanicals provided an invaluable reference tool as well.

The Gin Spider Diagram (GSD)

You'll recall that Chapter One provided a list of bases that gins typically have. Chapter Two extended this concept by considering the gins as still charges for use in a copper still.

With the botanicals there is juniper, front and centre, followed by coriander, perhaps angelica root and cardamom, followed by a citrus flavour. It could be any one of lime, lemon, orange, grapefruit or, indeed, any citrus product that you feel would contribute to the gin that you're looking to produce.

The Gin Spider Diagram (GSD) helps to assess the intensity levels of gin. The best way to kick off its use is to sample several examples of your favourite gins. Consider each of the major components that each gin possesses, albeit in differing quantities.

For simplicity, focus and ease of use, the six key characteristics to consider are:

- Juniper

- Herbal

- Floral

- Spirited (or alcoholic)

- Citrus

- Spicy (peppery or heated)

Grouping each characteristic type and sensation in this manner makes it easier to compare relative intensity on a scale rated from one to four; four being the most intense, one the least. I've used one to cover off characteristics that are too difficult to discern instead of zero by design.

Why one and not zero?

Purely to assist with the visual presentations to come.

Do not be surprised if you find that a gin with a known, specific botanical proves challenging to discern. In this case, put your experiences with water and blending to use by reducing the gin's strength by a quarter, and try again. This assessment may take some time to master but it is time well spent.

Here is my assessment of Roku™, a magnificent gin hailing from the Land of the Rising Sun.[50] It is beautifully presented with clear links to Japanese heritage paying homage to six key botanicals: yuzu peel, sencha tea (green tea), gyokuro tea (refined green tea), sakura flower (cherry blossom), sakura leaf (cherry leaves) and sansho pepper. The key observation lies with balance. Herbal – unsurprisingly – is the standout, but it's the balance across the other characteristics that makes Roku a joy to consume. Grab yourself a bottle and enjoy this oriental gem.

---

50 https://suntory.co.jp/wnb/rokugin/en

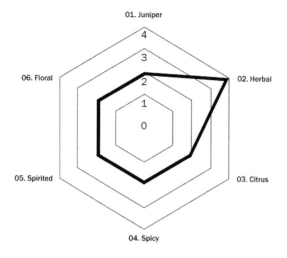

01. Juniper

06. Floral

02. Herbal

05. Spirited

03. Citrus

04. Spicy

GSD for herbal profile

GSD and testing

Assessment tools like this are far and away the most visually interesting tools to add to your gin testing arsenal. They provide an excellent way to qualitatively assess the balance between various botanicals in each gin. This also helps any up and coming gin maker to develop their knowledge of the botanicals and their interactions with one another. It provides a simple visual representation of what your olfactory super powers are trying to tell you.

Here is a list of three well-known gins and their respective lists of botanicals. Working with classic enduring brands will provide a good anchor point for future reference.

As you work through these gins, note the common botanicals they possess; juniper, angelica, coriander, lemon, orris root. This is a clear demonstration of the first two of the 3Bs – Botanicals and Bases – described in Chapter One, and how this approach to gin making has spanned centuries.

Beefeater, 1876 – a popular classic whose legacy spans centuries, with eight botanicals:

- Almond, angelica root, coriander, juniper, lemon, liquorice, orange, and orris root.

Bombay Sapphire, 1981 – a modern day 'reboot' of an eighteenth-century gin, with ten botanicals:

- Almond
- Angelica root
- Cassia
- Coriander
- Cubeb pepper
- Grains of paradise
- Juniper
- Lemon
- Liquorice
- Orris root

Hendrick's, 1999 – a late twentieth-century gin best described as a modern-day classic, with thirteen botanicals:

- Angelica root
- Caraway
- Chamomile
- Coriander
- Cubeb pepper
- Cucumber
- Elderflower
- Juniper
- Lemon
- Orange
- Orris root
- Rose
- Yarrow

The botanical listings for each gin provide all budding gin makers with invaluable insights concerning their flavour characteristics. There are diverse ways to develop the flavour profiles which draw similarities to culinary skills and techniques.

This also becomes clearer when considering gin manufacturing and production methods.

The key to bear in mind is this. Given a known list of botanicals, a gin sample provides the best opportunity to reflect and develop your olfactory super powers significantly faster.

Approach the assessment for each gin in the way described under the Test step in the D.I.S.T.I.L. process:

- Aroma

- Initial taste

- Palate

- After taste

Experience, record and note the aromas, tastes and flavours using simple language to describe the characteristics for each gin. Embed this as a habit each time you have the chance to try a gin. If you're out and about, use your phone to record your thoughts. Voice recordings work just fine for you to reference later. If you become well immersed in the assessment process, consider engaging a transcription service to collate your thoughts and commit them to print for future reference.

You'll recall the Testing step in the D.I.S.T.I.L. process in Chapter Two.

Apply the Testing steps and record your observations in your A5 notebook.

Water selections

You will recall from Chapter One that water is the dark horse of gin making. There is water for gin distillation, gin manufacturing, and gin testing.

For this exercise collect three or four samples of bottled water. If you have a filtration system available to you, then include this in the array of water samples.

The water may be at room temperature or chilled. The water temperature is not a show-stopper. The key is that water samples be at the same temperature and treated the same way for each case.

Small scale blends with water

Before you begin unleashing water upon your unsuspecting gin samples, here are a few process terms used in blending. The final volume in each case below will change and so will the alcoholic strength.

- Adding water to alcohol is a process called reduction; this will generate heat.

- Adding alcohol to water is a process called fortification; this will generate heat.

- Adding alcohol to alcohol is a process called compounding.

Let's use water at room temperature, meaning that the gins should be at room temperature as well. This means that the samples will be attemperated:

- Select one of the gins and set up a glass for each water sample.

- Dispense a shot of the gin into each wine glass.

- Take one of the water samples and dispense a shot of water into the first glass; cover the glass.

- Repeat this exercise with the other water samples.

- Let the samples stand where they are for 2–3 minutes.

- You are now aware that condensation will occur at the bottom of the watch glass. This will become quickly apparent and there will be some heat generation as well.

Assessing the gin blend

After 2–3 minutes uncover the glass and swirl the gin/water mix again.

Place the rim of the glass to your top lip beneath your nose but don't breathe in. The key to this step lies in allowing the aromas to meet you. Avoid any temptation to forcibly draw the aromas into your nose by inhaling; allow the aromas to rise and meet you as you swirl the glass.

Another way to achieve the same outcome is to hold the glass in one hand and then to wave your hand over the open top of the glass; the aromas will arise to meet you. This is a similar technique to one that chefs will use when assessing sauces, soups and other dishes. Gently waft the aromas toward you so that you're not overloading your olfactory super powers.

Assessment and record keeping

Once you've completed these activities for the first sample, write down what you think in your A5 note-book. For example, can you discern the juniper coming through? How about coriander? What about the angelica? Can you pick out any fruit flavours? Repeat this exercise for each gin you have at your disposal. Take a 2–3-minute break before starting the next assessment.

Bases and common ground

The focus of the exercise is to consider five main characteristics only; these are common characteristics in all gin and provide the basis for comparison. This is a chance to put the earlier section concerning Objective Reasoning to use.

The gins use a similar array of botanicals in most cases most of the time. Each gin maker will treat their botanical selections in diverse ways to distinguish themselves from one another. Any additional botanicals that distillers select are in place to provide the support act that sets each gin apart.

This key concept provides the means to understand what happens when distillers unlock the base botanicals. Once you have this concept in place, it will provide you with insights concerning the botanicals that you may choose for your gin.

You are still designing your own gin but chances are it will bring the characteristics common to some well-known gins to bear.

Consider gins from the 'old world' – Gordon's, Beefeater, Booths and Tanqueray. Now is a wonderful time to contrast these gin giants with contemporaries such as Hendrick's, The Botanist, Bloom, Hernö, Four Pillars, Aviation, Scapegrace, Poor Toms and Long Table.

These are all wonderful examples of modern gin, using advanced manufacturing and distilling techniques. The range, scope and scale of the gin firmament is vast and expanding, yet still pays homage to common bases.

GSD Basics – The Gin Spider Diagram in action

Now is a fun time to visualise your observations in a simple illustration based on the following six characteristics:

- Juniper

- Herbal

- Citrus

- Spiciness

- Spiritedness

- Floral

In short, it's a way to visually describe or represent what your olfactory super powers are telling you. What it says about your own perceptions concerning known brands and the way they've been put together, provides you with a simple, low-cost start to help build up your knowledge of gin, its components, and how they all relate together.

Here is a blank version of the GSD for you to sketch in your A5 notebook for starters. If you happen to have a few basic MS Excel skills or know someone who does, then it is a simple matter to input data and create your own GSDs.

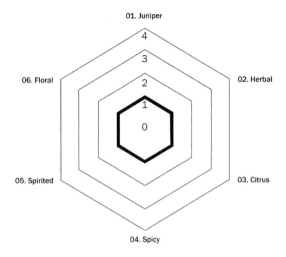

The blank GSD

The key to the GSD lies with answering a simple question for each characteristic in turn:

On a scale from 1–4 with 1 being 'absent' and 4 being 'High' describe/rate the level of intensity.

- Does the gin present a strong juniper aroma? This is characteristic of London Dry Gin styles in the main.

- Does the gin present a floral nose? This is a characteristic in many contemporary gins.

- Does the gin come across as strongly alcoholic? This is characteristic of many Navy strength gins and different alcohol base materials (for example, grain, whey, sugar).

- Does the gin take you slightly aback as you imbibe the aroma? This may be due to peppery tones in the nose or a strong alcoholic characteristic.

Once you make these discernments rate their intensity.

These experiences will help hone your olfactory super powers quickly. As always, note down your observations in your A5 notebook. Here are the questions posed for the Roku example described earlier.

GIN VISUALISATION TOOL – ASSESSMENT FOR:	ROKU		
No. ▼	Question ▼	Guidance ▼	Score ▼
1	Describe / rate the level of juniper intensity	01. Absent 02. Minor Level 03. Moderate Level 04. High Level	2
2	Describe / rate the level of herbal intensity	01. Absent 02. Minor Level 03. Moderate Level 04. High Level	4
3	Describe / rate the level of citrus intensity	01. Absent 02. Minor Level 03. Moderate Level 04. High Level	2
4	Describe / rate the level of spiciness intensity	01. Absent 02. Minor Level 03. Moderate Level 04. High Level	2
5	Describe / rate the level of alcohol intensity	01. Absent 02. Minor Level 03. Moderate Level 04. High Level	2
6	Describe / rate the level of floral intensity	01. Absent 02. Minor Level 03. Moderate Level 04. High Level	2

Gin visualisation tool assessment for Roku

All being well you will create a set of visual representations for each gin; here are some examples for your
records and future reference.

Here are my interpretations of several well-known
gins, expressed as GSDs. Everyone's palate is different so to that extent, there is no right or wrong answer.
What this exercise does help to achieve, is to focus
your own senses upon:

- The different expressions that each botanical
  brings to the product

- Your own way of experiencing how these
  stimulate your olfactory super powers

Try to compare your findings with the GSDs I've produced. If any of your assessments differ apply your
sense of relentless curiosity by seeking to understand
why this may be so. But remember the key rule: when
it comes to differences at this early stage of your gin
making journey, there is neither a right nor a wrong
answer, there is only the best answer.

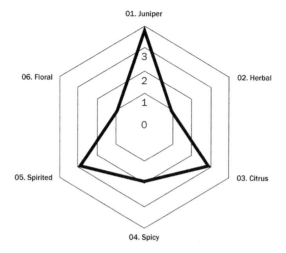

GSD for Beefeater

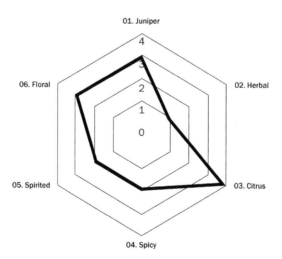

GSD for Bombay Sapphire

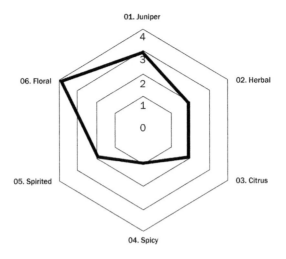

01. Juniper

02. Herbal

03. Citrus

04. Spicy

05. Spirited

06. Floral

GSD for Hendrick's

Revisiting the D.I.S.T.I.L. process

Testing

The next part of this exercise – the least glamorous part as you know from the T step in D.I.S.T.I.L. – is to taste test the gins. You will recall from Chapter One that gin tasting comprises four parts requiring your olfactory super powers; aroma and three tasting steps.

The first taste is important so it's best practice to describe the sensations you experience whenever you first taste the gin. The second part is when you swirl the gin within your mouth.

Allow the botanical flavours to play and develop upon your tongue; you may even experience a tingling or stinging feeling across parts of your tongue, particularly around the edges. That's a combination of the alcohol working on your taste buds, the interaction of the botanicals that are in the gin, and the formation of hydrogen bonds between the gin and your saliva.

Finally, swirl the gin before spitting it out into a spittoon. There will be residual aftertastes coming through that are noteworthy. As always, note your observations in your A5 notebook and illustrate any other thoughts you may have.

To recap:

It's the initial taste when you first imbibe the gin.

It's the mouth feel or the secondary taste that you get when you're swirling the gin upon your tongue. Allow the residues to cover your taste buds and to produce that tertiary taste sensation.

Finally swirl the gin before spitting it out into a spittoon; now assess the gin's aftertaste. The length of aftertaste or finish is often what sets many gins apart. This describes the body coming through with the gin. The aftertaste provides a measure of the care a distiller takes to ensure that each botanical is represented in a balanced fashion; each has its moment to shine, be it at the start, in the middle, the end or indeed from start to finish.

Combining these assessments means you can now record your observations as a visual record using a GSD.

These are representations of the gin's aroma and taste. The visual nature of the GSD makes it easy to understand the assessments of botanical groupings and intensity.

What you can then do is twofold. You now understand the gins you've tried; this in turn presents an opportunity to compare botanical interactions between products that are made differently.

Create GSDs

Recall from Chapter One that there were five types of gin made using a pre-distillation technique called steeping. You can now assess these gins and create GSDs for each of them.

There are variations between each of them both in terms of the additional botanicals put to use and botanical quantities.

By creating GSDs for these gins, you can visualise the interactions between the different base components as well. In other words, you can see how relative botanical quantities – the magic ratios – respond to different quantities of juniper berry, coriander seed, angelica and cardamom.

In a more specific example, you can now visualise and describe the influence crushed cardamom has on a gin when compared with whole cardamom.

This is one case where there are several subtleties and nuances which bring depth and texture to the gins that we're looking to produce.

Why is juniper so special?

From Chapter One you now know that the steeping process is a start. This is the simplest way to develop a feel for how the ingredients behave. It is also an approach with the best chance of success at the least cost.

These gins are steeped and by modern standards have room for improvement. They represent the targets we are aiming for and provide a knowledge base for understanding the interactions between botanicals. That is a key concept in all product development efforts.

Having said that, we cannot overstate how important the steeping process is. It is a legitimate predistillation process that is used extensively by operations around the world.

For example, Poor Toms Fool Strength gin – a recent gold medal winner at the International Wine and Spirit Competition (IWSC) in 2018 – uses a steeping process prior to distillation, as does Sipsmith Very Junipery Over Proof™.

Each of these products treats juniper by steeping the berries in a warmed alcohol-water solution for 12 hours. This creates specific nuances and kick-starts the gin's depth of flavour before the distillation takes place.

Some distillers add even more juniper through direct addition into the still charge or via a cage in the still column. In the latter case the resulting vapour steams the juniper berries under reflux, enriching the vapour and distillates prior to collection.

The rate limiting step in steeping operations lies with the protracted time required. These process descriptions also demonstrate that if you treat a specific botanical – in this case, juniper berries – differently and with respect, you can drive amazing levels of flavour depth and development.

Juniper berries lend themselves to these treatment variations very well; hardy with lots of flavour potential. See if you can think of other botanicals that you could use, that are hardy, flavoursome and heat tolerant.

The juniper berry structure makes it a suitable candidate for these different processes. It comprises three seeds within the husk. Each of those three seeds has several flavour components called terpenes.

These are naturally occurring items in nature, with many of these compounds present in juniper berries. The list of items is diverse but includes the following common items:

- Camphor – often used in mothballs, this has a distinctive aroma

- Alpha pinene – the source of the pine needle aroma that juniper berries exude

Collectively these compounds create a flavour combination that is greater than the sum of the parts. A cluster of compounds exist within juniper's three seeds, housed by a berry husk.

If you were to create a still charge with these berries alone, you already have an array of flavour dimensions available which you can build upon.

The berries' interactions under reflux can lead to interesting flavour outcomes. The ways you treat juniper berries – through direct heat, steeping, steaming, or reflux processes – has a different effect upon the berry itself. This means that there are exciting possibilities based on the way you treat the botanicals.

3Bs and the five bases

If you're looking for a level of intensity, revisit the 3Bs, consider the five bases, magic ratios, the GSDs you have created, and the notes you have for each. Look at the array of resources you have at your disposal!

Intensity is based on your own research and applying what you've learnt. From the sample GSDs you can see that Roku has high herbal intensity, Hendrick's high floral, and Beefeater high juniper.

Further, you know what their respective botanical listings are, so you can immediately apply what you've learnt from these. And test. Test again, and then test some more.

Simplicity is key. Treating the gin making process simply can produce an endless scope for variation and imagination. One of the wonderful things about gin's global upsurge today lies in the fact that people are limited solely by their imaginations.

There was a time when a sense of secrecy and guardianship around gin making tended to limit and constrain creativity. That still exists to some extent because of the long-standing traditions associated with traditional brands. But as people have taken on a more contemporary approach to an old art, it's now a case of transparency and working together. Collaboration is the key to success these days. As a 1980s veteran it's a heartening development for all the right reasons.

People now willingly share their ideas, providing good sounding boards as a result. They'll provide a basis to help you every step of the way and I'm no different. I'm happy to help a lot of people who are willing to take on this art and craft. It's been around for hundreds of years, so it's well worth promoting and protecting from here on in. Gin makers have no desire to bring this to an end for any reason whatsoever.

CHAPTER FOUR

My Challenge to You

You've taken a rollicking ride over Chapter One and Chapter Two of this book, and then delved into a more detailed application of gin making and testing in Chapter Three. Given the welter of information at your disposal you can be well excused thinking that now is the perfect time for a refreshing drink! You've certainly earned it as far as I can tell. I for one would be both receptive and supportive of rewarding yourself like this, on the proviso that your drink of choice is one which showcases juniper as the star.

You will recall from Chapter Two, the last step of the D.I.S.T.I.L. process referred to Launch. This may have been the last step in the process but more importantly it was an invitation for you to consider this seemingly simple two-fold question, the answer to which may change over time:

'What is the best launch decision for me right now?'

There were four launch options, two related to a commercial venture (Solopreneur or Joint Venture), the other two considered gin making as a hobby or sideline interest (solo or family and friends).

My challenge to you is to consider if your interest is a sideline/hobby or a potential commercial venture. You have a grasp of the basics ranging from steeping to an initial approach to small scale distillation. You may not have realised this at the time, but the passage from Chapter One to Chapter Two was a step-change in both scale and speed. This is no accident; this approach has a proven track record of success in efforts to get to this pivotal stage; to commercialise or not. In a sense, it is akin to reaching base camp before making an assault on a mountain summit.

Distilled gin – from concept to commercialisation

After many years of working experience in a diverse array of industries and roles, its staggering how often the same type of problem presents itself as an opportunity to solve. Every solution must have the following characteristics to improve the likelihood for a successful outcome.

A remarkable and complete solution delivers:

1. Clarity

2. Certainty

3. Peace of mind

When it comes to gin-making, the 3Bs describe a series of building blocks that form a solid foundation for the work to come.

The D.I.S.T.I.L. process applies the 3B building blocks in pursuit of the remarkable and complete solution to gin making: quality, quantity, scalability and speed.

Launching a gin product for commercialisation is a team sport and one of my specialities. Partnering with a trusted authority can help deliver a complete and remarkable solution. There are few things more satisfying for a distiller than helping budding gin makers plan, schedule, finance and apply the next steps required for scalability, compliance and commercialisation. There are 200 or more challenges that end-to-end commercialisation will attract; the good news is that every one of these challenges has a solution. The most challenging part is getting started.

Let me explain why.

Pretty well anyone can distil gin once you know what you need to distil and how to do so. However, distilling gin isn't the type of commercial vocation that you can throw together at the last minute. It takes a significant amount of time and effort to determine for example, your botanical selection, the size of the charge; in other words, the amount of alcohol that you're going to use and understanding how your still works. You're trying to understand the nuances when you first get underway. Any sort of new machinery or new set of botanicals takes time to work through. Even things like weather temperature differences can have an effect on the performance of a still. Once you've got process control down pat, it becomes pretty well smooth sailing.

That leaves at least another 198 things to consider!

Ultimately what it comes down to is that you can distil as much gin as you like, but the market generally determines whether you're successful or not.

A simple score card can assist you with determining if you are ready to take the next step to commercialisation. My example score card provides a set of questions in three specific areas (scale, risk and value) with four responses available for each question. The output resembles the following illustrations and can help you to determine your own answer to the question, '*What is the best Launch decision for me right now?*'

I have included a small sample of the scorecard for illustrative purposes only. In this value proposition, there is a set of twenty-two questions with a series of four answers for each question. The questions cover seven areas of concern:

1. Making money

2. Levels of investment

3. Impact

4. Work-life balance

5. Time investment

6. Team size

7. Operational risk

Baseline Assessments

Sideline interest

Initial assessment in this output suggests that the product scale is more aligned to be a sideline interest. Commercial Launch is not the right thing to do right now.

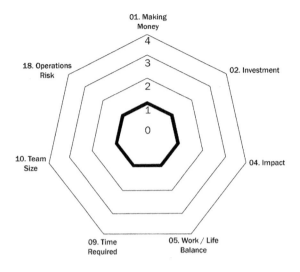

Distilling ventures: hobby or business – 0

Commercial interest

Initial assessment in this output suggests that the product scale is aligned to a venture that is more than a sideline. Commercial Launch may well be the right thing to do right now.

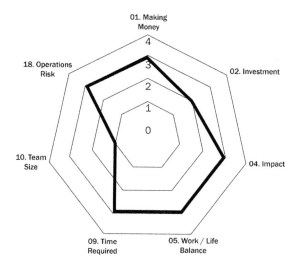

Distilling ventures: hobby or business – 2.57

What is clear from the answers provided, is that you and your team understands that there is:

- 02. Investment – a reasonable level of investment required

- 04. Impact – it will be major change to the way people work right now

- 05. Work/Life Balance – running the business day to day will be time consuming

- 10. Team Size – the team is not large

- 18. Operations Risk – there is significant operational risk

- 01. Making Money – there is a good chance of making money

In other words, this will be a new venture, requiring a change to the team's current employment arrangements.

Here is a list of areas that need due consideration when embarking upon a venture such as this:

- Plant materials
- Buildings
- Receipt and storage of alcoholic products
- Packaging components
- Water for reduction
- Product preparation
- Filtration
- Bottling
- Storage/despatch
- Record keeping
- Finished goods inventory
- Materials requirements planning
- Bills of material
- Financial reconciliation
- Team building

Here is a sample list of the questions you will need to consider when deciding to take on this challenge.

- Where will I set up my distillery?

- What packaging equipment do I need? Can I hire it?

- What are my energy requirements – eg gas, three-phase electricity, solar panels?

- How will I treat trade waste?

- What will I do with spent botanicals?

- Who will do what and when (division of labour, roles and responsibilities)?

- Who will provide operational, sales and financial reports?

- What size still do I purchase? How many?

- Where is my water supply?

- What plant do I need to use water that is fit for purpose?

- How will I measure volume, strength and weight?

- What documentation will I need on hand to satisfy compliance needs?

- Where will I store my botanicals?

- How will I determine supplier agreements for botanicals?

- What licences will I need (eg manufacturing, dangerous goods)?

- What planning compliance do I need to satisfy local authorities?

- What insurances do I need?

- Will I have permission to sell gin on site?

- What safety and legal measures do I need in place to store, manage and transport alcohol products?

- What Food Safety criteria need satisfaction prior to sale (eg labelling, contents, volumes, tamper-proof closures)?

This is by no means exhaustive or complete, but it does serve as a guide to the complexities that you and your team will need to take on. A leadership team with a mixture of skills such as engineering, finance, property, legal, technical, manufacturing fast moving consumer goods (FMCG), supply chain, sales, and marketing has the makings to set up an operation for success.

There are many areas to consider but if you know what they are, then planning solutions becomes a simpler matter. This means that investment in expert help adds value in the form of clarity, certainty and peace of mind. It also means that if you come across an unexpected development, you can tackle these with confidence too. The approach to Objective Reasoning in preparation for Chapter Two comes into its own in these cases.

Closing Remarks

And that's it. You've taken a distiller's tour around the gin making firmament from its modest beginnings, taking in a sensory experience that is hundreds of years in the making.

Gin's journey, first prompted by a seventeenth century monarch, to the modern-day environment of sociability and real-time connectedness is simply remarkable. It's endured 300 years so far and is not going away any time soon. I think you will agree that gin is still magic, despite this passage of time.

That's Heritage.

With relentless curiosity at your disposal, there are so many areas you can explore in your gin making journey. By emulating the energy, desire and enthusiasm of those that have gone before, you will become tantalisingly close to producing something special. When you get there treasure it, guard it and nurture it.

That's Guardianship.

Today's enthusiasts are forging an exciting future. Count yourself among this group of intrepid creators and take up the challenge. Gin is undergoing a global renaissance, hitherto unseen since seventeenth- and eighteenth-century London, fuelled by people just like you.

That's Legacy.

This book demonstrates the accessibility you have to the basic tools of the trade, the magic that stills bring to bear and gin making's similarities with diverse creative pursuits.

My hope is that my writing has proven useful to you and that it helps fuel the fire you have within to create something unique and special. In other words, take 300 years of gin making heritage and create your legacy. Continue your journey at www.stillmagic.net

Glossary

Alcoholic strength	Measure of per cent alcohol by volume. Stated as ABV or alc/vol it must be measured by a method approved by the local regulatory body.
Alcoholic volume	Measure as litres of absolute alcohol. Express in LAL. It is the product of volume (in litres) multiplied by alcoholic strength at the appropriate local temperature.

Azeotrope	A mixture of two liquids with a boiling point that is lower than either component part. This is the heart of all distillation work and the basis for end-product purity. It comprises a mixture of some 96% alcohol and 4% water, boiling at 78.2 Celsius.
Bathtub Gin	Compounded gin (a style looked down upon by distillers, as the botanicals are steeped in high proof spirit rather than distilled).
Botanicals	The collective term to describe gin components of plant origin.
Closures	Fitments that are used to seal a bottle: ROPP – roll-on pilfer proof EST – external screw thread NRF – no refillable fitment Cork
Compounding	The use of full-strength alcohol to enhance and balance a gin's botanicals.

Congeners	This refers to small amounts of chemicals such as methanol, fusel alcohols, acetone, acetaldehyde, esters, tannins, and aldehydes that result from a fermentation process. Distillation processes endeavour to remove these via the heads (foreshot) fraction as these can adversely impact final product quality.
Craft gin	Small batch artisanal local gins.
Demineralisation	Purification of water in which the metals and their salts are removed.
Disgorged	Emptied.
Filling Temperature	Temperature at which the alcoholic product is filled.
Gas Chromatography (GC)	A technique used in analytical chemistry for separating and analysing compounds capable of vaporisation. Typical uses of GC include testing the purity of a particular substance, or separating the different components of a mixture. In some situations, GC may help in identifying a compound.

Genever	Original Dutch juniper spirit which led to the creation of this drink. It retains the flavour of the grains on which it was based.
Gin Pentagon	A visual assessment tool that illustrates the relative intensity of five gin descriptors on a scale from 1 to 3.
GSD	Gin Spider Diagram. A visual assessment tool illustrates the relative intensity of six gin characteristics using a scale from 1 to 4.
Hand-ball	Move or load by hand.
Heads	The initial distillate fraction that distillers collect but put aside. This fraction is often full of poor quality congeners such as methanol.
Heart	The distillate fraction that gin makers retain for use in gin production. The distiller's skill lies in their ability to determine when to start collecting the heat, and then when to stop.

Hydrometer	A device used to measure strength by suspension in alcohol. Coupled with using a thermometer, the raw measurements from the thermometer and hydrometer are corrected to 20°C.
In-line filtration	System of filtration in which the filtered product is bottled immediately after filtration.
Integrity	Maintaining the perfect state.
International Gins	These are mass-produced gins made in huge volumes.
London Dry	A style of gin that can be made anywhere in which juniper is the dominant botanical, and is made in the 'one shot' method. All the botanicals are added to the still, the distillation takes place, and then the gin is blended with water with nothing else added.

Modern Classic Gin	This category describes gins that are less-juniper and citrus-forward than a traditional London Dry, allowing other botanicals to contribute more readily to the flavour profile. They typically have most or all of their botanicals the same as a traditional London Dry, and may introduce a couple of novel botanicals. Examples are Aviation and Hendrick's Gin, as well as the majority of those described as 'contemporary'.
Modern Regional Gin	This is a type of gin that uses mostly local botanicals to make a gin that distinctly represents the local area. These gins still have a juniper backbone. Gins in this group include The Botanist, Four Pillars Rare Dry Gin, and Poor Toms Sydney Dry Gin.
Mother's Ruin	A term originating in seventeenth century London used to describe gin and its social impacts.

Navy Strength	Around 57% alcohol, developed because the British Navy used to keep gin next to the gunpowder, and to ensure that the gunpowder would still ignite if the gin spilt onto it.
Non-fillable fitment	Fitment that stops bottles from being refilled after the contents are consumed.
Objective Reasoning	A decision-making technique that compares and contrasts the relative merits of two or more options.
Old Tom Gin	A slightly sweeter style of gin, generally using slightly sweeter botanicals along with added sugar.
Organoleptic testing	Checking the aroma and taste of a liquid.
Passivate	Rendering a surface inert to an alcoholic product.
pH	A measure that describes the acidity of a liquid.
Pickled	Immersion in alcohol to remove odours, and to passivate surfaces.

Reduction	Lowering the alcoholic strength to that required for bottling.
Reverse Osmosis	A process that treats municipal water supplies for use in gin making.
SynGyn	A neologism for a synthetic product – Synthetic Gin – built from analytical grade extracts of juniper's most prominent flavour components.
Tails	The final distillate fraction that contains flavour compounds with high boiling points such as amyl alcohol. Distillers will put these aside as well for either additional treatment or licensed trade waste disposal.
Torque Tester	Equipment used to measure the amount of force required to break a ROPP when opening a bottle.
Vat	Storage tank

Acknowledgements

As you look to the future, acknowledging the past and present is an important premise in all of life's dealings. The following *whakataukī* (proverb) captures this sentiment elegantly:

> *'E taku mokai, he wa poto noa koe i waenganui i te wa kua hipa ki te wa kei te tu mai.'*[51]

> 'You are but a speck in the moment of time, situated between two eternities, the past and the future.'

I'd like to thank the following people:

---

51 Waereti Rolleston-Tait, April 1984.

Heritage

Mr Grainger Hannah and Cliff Jones, for taking a punt on a twenty-one-year-old science graduate all those years ago.

The still-house crew of Peter Tomlinson, Ian Hourigan-Johnston and Steve Warren. Your friendship, guidance, good humour and patience when showing me the right way to make distilled gin is something I – and now many others – will treasure for years to come. I'm now far better at crosswords, and still have no idea how to pick a winner in a one-horse race, but rest assured your gin legacy will endure.

Mr Peter Deane, Gordon's Gin, Laindon, for showing me how the pursuit for excellence starts at the beginning, by getting the basics right. Turn up on time; do as you're told.

All of you showed me that better people make better distillers.

Guardianship

Stephen Itzcovitz and Norman Hill, for onboarding me into the Australian team. The opportunity to develop the UDL range of premixed drinks, and premium offerings such as Dark & Stormy, XLR8, Johnnie

Walker and Cola, would not have been possible otherwise. Thank you.

David Marr, John Halmarick and Warrick Duthy, for convincing me that the spirits business in the South Pacific is exciting, vibrant and relevant. You were correct then, and nothing has changed in that regard.

To the Punja family and Ashok Kumar Bhatia. Thank you for the opportunity to help with your new gin, whisky and vodka operations in Lautoka. It was great fun from start to finish.

Dr Lou Muller, for your support in helping our business efforts to produce Bundaberg rum outside Australia for the first time.

Mr Terry Lee, for selecting me to take up a fantastic stint in Papua New Guinea. Making gin, rum, whisky and everything else in between was an unforgettable experience. KC OP rum is a legacy that disrupted an industry, generating unprecedented national interest and demand at every level. Opportunities that epitomise guardianship like this are rare indeed.

Legacy

Jesse and Griff, our story is another chapter in an odyssey whose best is yet to come. It's when moments become memories that clarity presents itself.

Cameron Mackenzie, humility with success, good humour and generosity writ large. I'm confident that your contributions and passion will ensure that gin's legacy is in good hands – because better people make better distillers.

Mary Thompson, for your enduring sense of practicality and acerbic wit, that helped me to improve the 3Bs and D.I.S.T.I.L. process descriptions. In all that life presents, there is no better practitioner of the 'less-is-more' concept than you my love.

Ella Frances Barrett, Emily Kate Barrett, Juno Hana Gamble, Enso Finlay Gamble, I am blessed to have such fine *mokopuna*. When you're ready, come make gin with *Koro*.

Last, but certainly not least, any endeavour of this nature is a team sport, and *Still Magic* is no exception.

I'd like to thank the publication team at Rethink Press, Lucy McCarraher, Kathleen Steeden, Fern Labrum and Joe Gregory, whose collective mentorship and guidance brought my thoughts to print; my beta-readers, Astral Sligo, Judy Apps and Nichole Tudor, for demonstrating patience and objectivity by taking on a task that would drive most people to drink... maybe it did... on more than one occasion; finally, Julia Vale Gamble, Lauren Orrell and Simon Gamble, for your creativity, energy and stylish insights concerning design, presentation and resolving the technicalities that accompany creative expression.

The Author

Marcel Thompson (Ngāti Whātua, Waikato) is an award-winning gin maker whose career began in the 1980s, in New Zealand.

His unique skillset helps facilitate work with joint venture partnerships and start-ups, and commercialisation of new product concepts. This includes resolving the end-to-end technical challenges that often bedevil alcohol manufacturing facilities.

Innovation, problem solving, teamwork and servant leadership best describe the value he brings to those looking to make their mark.

Marcel's products have won a number of awards.

Product	Competition	Year	Award
Poor Toms Sydney Dry Gin	San Francisco Spirits Competition, San Francisco	2016	Silver
Poor Toms Sydney Dry Gin	San Francisco Spirits Competition, San Francisco	2017	Gold
Poor Toms Sydney Dry Gin	San Francisco Spirits Competition, San Francisco	2018	Bronze
Fool Strength Gin	San Francisco Spirits Competition, San Francisco	2018	Bronze
Fool Strength Gin	Australian Distilled Spirits Awards, Melbourne	2018	Gold
Fool Strength Gin	International Wines and Spirits Competition, London	2018	Gold

Contact details

⊕ www.stillmagic.net

🐦 Marcel@Still_Magic

in https://linkedin.com/in/marcel-thompson-62baa01

f https://facebook.com/marcelstillmagic

Printed in Great
Britain
by Amazon